#blacklove

#blacklove

The Intricacies and Intimacies of Romantic Love in Black Relationships

Edited by Tapo Chimbganda

LEXINGTON BOOKS
Lanham • Boulder • New York • London

Published by Lexington Books
An imprint of The Rowman & Littlefield Publishing Group, Inc.
4501 Forbes Boulevard, Suite 200, Lanham, Maryland 20706
www.rowman.com

6 Tinworth Street, London SE11 5AL

British Library Cataloguing in Publication Information Available

Library of Congress Cataloging-in-Publication Data

Names: Chimbganda, Tapo, editor.
Title: #blacklove : the intricacies and intimacies of romantic love in black relationships / edited by
     Tapo Chimbganda.
Other titles: Hashtag blacklove
Description: Lanham : Lexington Books, [2019] | Includes bibliographical references and index. |
     Summary: "This edited volume qualifies black love on the basis of black identity. Much of what
     is experienced of blackness as an identity arises out of a juxtaposition to other races and iden-
     tities, particularly whiteness. The contributors in this volume resist the idea of black love in
     reference to whiteness by exposing the hidden toxicities that come with a focus on whiteness.
     They reflect on intricate and intimate relationship dynamics that arise out of a violent and
     challenging past between Black women and Black men"-- Provided by publisher.
Identifiers: LCCN 2019041646 (print) | LCCN 2019041647 (ebook) | ISBN 9781793613820 (cloth) |
     ISBN 9781793613837 (epub) | ISBN 9781793613844 (pbk)
Subjects: LCSH: Man-woman relationships. | Blacks--Race identity. | Love. Classification: LCC
     HQ801.A3 B54 2019 (print) | LCC HQ801.A3 (ebook) | DDC 306.7--dc23
LC record available at https://lccn.loc.gov/2019041646
LC ebook record available at https://lccn.loc.gov/2019041647

My appreciation to all the contributors who took the time and put a significant piece of themselves in writing to make this book a worthwhile text. Heartfelt thanks and love to Dr. Daniel Antwi-Amoabeng, a big contributor in so many ways.

#blacklove has over 4.4 million tags on Instagram alone. On every social media platform, #blacklove is a constantly trending topic, which continues to draw the voices of both men and women all over the world. Oprah's show on Black love was very popular and continues to influence the conversation. Here are a few examples of what people have to say about #blacklove on twitter: Dedicated to all those striving for #blacklove and life. @dunnkhad1: I ran out of mental space for drama @onboardw_beauty: powerful, strong, consistent love like no other! @ynohtnaii: pouring into one another without hesitation. @gloryshered: That look of confidence amidst hostility

Table of Contents

Preface

There are three questions in any discussion of Black love. The most obvious and misleading is (1) *what is love?* The next two questions, equally crucial to any understanding of the first, but often never posed are (2) *who is the Black woman/man*; and (3) *who does she/he love?* Unless you inquire on who she is—her identity, intersectionality, culture, social standing, religion, motherhood, education, economics, and so many other factors—and *who* it is that she loves; unless you explore the inner workings and the essence of the one who is loving and who is loved, you are likely to conclude that Black love is fickle and irrational, given to self-destruction and self-mutilation, and it cannot endure the test of time.

This book qualifies Black love on the basis of Black identity and the love that rises out of that. It is true that much of what we understand of Blackness as an identity arises out of a juxtaposition to other races and multiple cultures, particularly whiteness. Like Fanon (2008) said, a Black man must be Black in reference to whiteness; and Blackness has no ontological resistance to whiteness (paraphrased). And yet, what the brave people in this book have done is resist that idea of Black love in reference to whiteness by uncovering the hidden toxicities that come with a focus on whiteness. They have shared their struggles and revealed their battle scars so that Black love can qualify on its own merit as something to long for, something to dream of, something to imagine because of its intricate and intimate value. White supremacy is indeed an ugly undercurrent, like a mold growing in between the walls, under floor boards and in the attic, slowly poisoning the Black family, who in ignorance continue to struggle with numerous mental and emotional health issues. Whiteness causes Black love to cough and wheeze, its immune system compromised, as an overwhelming sense of fatigue and lethargy takes over, eventually leading to physical pain. The contributors in this book have all uncovered signifiers in their own stories that speak of a life compromised by racism and a love so tender and bruised by oppression that it is a miracle they still seek it.

However, can we and should we lay all the blame for the disintegration of the Black family and the desolation of Black love on White supremacy, racism, and its vicissitudes? At what point does the Black woman or the Black man take responsibility for the relationship they have built? Whose job is it to teach Black children how to love and be loved? In this book you will find critical questions for Black women and men to answer. Black adults must stand for something they might never have experienced because their parents could not teach them. The writers believe that there is a way, many ways, for Black love to triumph over its past and present challenges. They envision a way for Black love to take up the mantle of endurance and commitment, a way for Black love to survive, strive, and thrive despite everything. They have shared their perspectives and offered insight into the anatomy of Black love. May you find hope for your own love, wisdom to help your loved ones, and understanding to sustain your relationship.

Introduction

The man I love is proud. He walks with his back so straight and head so high, he takes over any space. He is just over five feet and nine inches tall, but his pride makes him tower over others. They tell him he is domineering and speaks too aggressively because he speaks in an animated way, with his entire body. He is an African-born man who has become a Black man in North America. He holds his head high and keeps his back straight, resisting the bend that comes from the attitudes and prejudices of his non-Black colleagues, who question his every decision and use adjectives like "little" and yet look at him like a violent perpetrator. He is Asante and when he says his name, he tilts his chin a little to the heavens. Raised in Africa, when he talks of his ancestors, he speaks of warriors, proud men of the golden stool, elegant women of royal blood lines, and wise matriarchs who raised their children to be spiritual.

In my experience, to love a Black man is not easy because his life is not easy. On many days, when he comes home from work, my partner and I discuss his colleagues', patients', and bosses' microaggressions and blatant racism. We drink a cup of tea trying to understand the nurse who tells him his name frustrates her and she's tired of trying to say it. We make dinner pondering the colleague who tells him he needs an attitude adjustment because he asked for clarity on a plan of care for a critically ill patient. We sit side by side, laughing at the old White man who tells him he would rather consult with the doctor, even though he is his doctor. We have logged many hours, debriefing on his day so that these incidents and occurrences can be invalidated in our lives and he can go to work, do his job, care for sick people, tolerate abrasive attitudes, and maintain his smile in the face of constant testing. He does smile a lot, an observation the same people who view him as aggressive have made in rare moments of camaraderie.

Their attitudes have created a need in our relationship that must be fulfilled. I am conscious of this as I endeavor to privilege him in the space that is our relationship. I love a man who is the target of low self-esteemed White people who cannot understand why a Black man, nay, an African, is the doctor whom they must depend on for healthcare. This is how I must show him love: our relationship is many things, including the container for racial frustrations and outrage. Our relationship is the privileged space, where we create humor out of abrasive incidents and crack jokes about the absurdity of the racist mind. I choose to show my love for this man by accepting his version of work related conflict. Where he is told, "not everything is about race," I ask him, "Was it a White woman who said that?" My man is handsome, smart, and so compassionate; and these are the things on which I focus. In our relationship, he is king, and he is honored not only because he deserves it but because that is what it is to privilege another. I express gratitude because he actively takes care of me and provides for me. I express gratitude that he always shows up for me, and I appreciate his heart, which is bigger than everything else. The man I love is proud and I am mightily proud of him.

Me, I am a Bantu woman. Born and raised in Africa to see myself as more than what racism says I am. I am fierce, and I am bold. I love the same way. So, I love this Black man who cannot and will not shrink himself to accommodate the oppression that demands he must be something else. I have become a prayer warrior:

> *Jesus, give him the strength to smile when he should roar.*
> *Father, give him the grace to cross his arms when he should stand his ground.*
> *Lord, give him the wisdom to rise above when he should strike down.*

Every morning, I pray that someone will not ruin his life with racial garbage and absurd bigotry.

Like so many Black people, for me faith is a shelter from the tornadoes and hurricanes that racism beats against my relationship. Sometimes, I question God, why is racism such a powerful enemy in the lives of so many who believe in loving their neighbors as they do themselves. But faith offers answers to other questions, not the ones I have; and God in his infinite wisdom makes me strong where racism would make me weak. That is what I believe.

In her chapter, "The Black Man's Search for God," Carissa McCray shares a heartbreaking search for divinity that will answer the questions of Black men lost and estranged from their ancestors and from their spiritual selves. They seek a religion that will restore the lost and wayward fathers, gratify their struggling mothers and wives, and protect their vulnerable families. In their search for this god, disillusioned and traumatized, they become gods themselves and as every god must have worshippers, they turn their desires on the women in their lives and indoctrinate their children to follow in their beliefs. The pain and further trauma that ensues can only further alienate and destroy the spirits of Black families. For the Black woman who wants to love and build with her man, the gulf between them widens because he has become a god unable to connect with his supposed-to-be-worshipper. McCray's first-person account, freed from academic or theoretical complication and interpretation, is a simple narrative that shines a light on the bastardization of Black Christians in White religion. How can Black people believe in the same God as their oppressors? Should Black people return to their ancestral worship and seek to reconnect with higher powers in other ways? These are some of the questions that arise from her story, which she shares to elicit a spiritual reflection on what we believe as Black people and why we believe these things. How can we love when we don't believe or how can we believe and love when the two seem incompatible?

One might say that racism has taught me to love unconditionally and to privilege a flawed being. The history of colonialism and the vicissitudes of racism have eroded the privilege of men and women in society and unfortunately that condition has extended into their love lives and marriages resulting in broken homes and estranged children who grow up to repeat the cycle. Do my partner and I have an advantage because we were raised in Africa? Perhaps, but the diaspora has taken its toll on what we came with to this part of the world. Some days are difficult. Days when we both have racist inflicted wounds to lick. Then who can contain the others hurts, frustrations, and disappointments? In those moments we struggle to be together because looking into each other's eyes we see the pain that will leave an ugly scar.

I'll be honest, as a Black woman in love, I am, at times, reluctant to see the flaws in my relationship. I cling to it because it provides me the space to work through the trauma of racism and the complexities of blackness. Speaking as one who has dated other races, I find my Black love to be protective and empowering. At the same time, I admit there are issues that go unresolved for too long that have nothing to do with race and society and have everything to do with who we are as individuals. As all couples do, we have differences that arise out of our childhood and upbringing that cultivate expectations that the other views as unreasonable. Because some days all we can do is go to bed content in the knowledge that we have overcome yet another incident of racism and its trauma, we are blinded to other termites eating away at our foundation.

Similarly, Jade Benn, in "Black British Women, Love, and Politics of Choice," admits there were choices she made for the wrong reasons and focuses she kept erroneously. For her, the road to recovery and self-healing was difficult but she is the better for it. She illustrates that for Black women there is a danger of misplaced strength, commitment, and love for which we must be accountable. Is it the fault of Black men if we keep getting hurt or do we at some point need to take charge of our own love and give it to ourselves? How can Black men love us when we cannot love ourselves? Have we been so hurt and let down in the past, we have stopped expecting good and wholesome love from our partners? Why do we even try if we are not investing in a good relationship through our words and actions? What will it take for us to nurture better love for ourselves?

Michael Baugh, in "Emotional Storms and Black Intimacies," offers a reflective uncovering of the wounds that racism inflicts on Black couples sending them reeling in destructive patterns that separate and alienate so that they never really know each other. He confesses he never really knew his mother who spent her life being a "strong Black woman." She was so strong that her husband found no reason to empower her. Instead, he took up the "cool Black man" pose. His pose benefited strangers but alienated his wife who saw no reason to pour her love into an absent man. Michael's description of his parent's coupling leaves one questioning where the child might find emotional nourishment when the parents have created an environment so arid and hardened that love refuses to grow. In poetic rhythms of passion and pain spent recklessly; of sourness and soreness left carelessly; Michael forces us to reflect on our treatment of each other as Black couples. Why if I see my man sinking must I stamp him further into the ground? Why when he sees me struggling must he remove his support, leaving me to dangle precariously in hopelessness? If he and I, as Black people, know the burden that racism has forced us to carry, why do we not privilege each other and lend each other strength so that we can build a strong home? Isn't that what Black love should do?

As a people, Black folks are strong. We must be. Our love must be stronger than the pressures all couples face. But in our determination to be strong have we also hardened our hearts against each other in those moments of discord? Have we foreclosed the pain of partners that we no longer see as compatible with our ideals? Have Black men chosen to protect their egos and pride at the expense of Black women? Have Black women chosen to negate the pain of their men and see only what they fail to be? The tensions between the sexes seem to expand with each generation. How are we not healing? Why do we not see what is at stake? When we allow Whiteness and systems of White supremacy to come between us, we risk turning on each other and turning away from the Black love that could be our saving grace. "'What's Love Got to Do with It?'—A Piece for the Brothas" Evelyn Amponsah insists Black men interrogate their desire to keep Black women in positions of disadvantage while they take advantage of the patriarchal and racist systems of oppression. She questions why, if a Black man knows the pain of racism, he would turn his back on the Black woman and see her as flawed in preference to a White woman. Is the Black woman bitter? Is she angry? Is she desperate? Or is she simply holding Black men accountable for the pain they inflict on Black women? Using pop cultural references, Evelyn speaks as only a scorned Black woman can do to a wayward Black man who has lost his way—with truth, honesty, passion, courage, compassion, and a hint of righteous indignation.

The question is: where did the tension between Black men and Black women come from? What causes us to turn on each other? Who created and propagates this narrative? I've had arguments with my partner that left me genuinely confounded and confused. These arguments rise out of histories that we do not share, and impressions left by others. One time, he uttered a negative and generalized statement about women. I looked at him, "But I am the woman who is here, with you! Is that what you think of me?" We had a discussion then about his attitudes and views of women. It was a place from which he had to move in order to see me as I am, not as he has experienced with others. An imperative challenge is to examine these contentions and trace them to their origin. Whether we do it together or separately, it must be done. Media has a lot to do with how we come to understand the Black community outside of our immediate circles and it has much to do with our impressions of the opposite sex. Unfortunately, media is still not a friend to Black people. At a time when social justice is forcing remediation from a very reluctant White system, we need to be aware and address the harmful images and content that for decades flashed across our television screens miseducating us on issues of love, sex, and marriage in the Black community.

Riché Richardson in "No Longer 'Obsolete' and 'Dangerous,' but Still Single: Black Masculinity and Marriage in African American Film at the Dawn of the Twenty-First Century" examines dominant themes in African American films in the millennial era that highlighted friendship groups of Black men as characters and foregrounded their struggles related to love relationships and marriage. Including productions such as *The Best Man*, *The Brothers*, and *Head of State*, she also highlights the issues of Black psychological interiority and the ways which such films recurrently depicted educated, middle class, professional Black women as undesirable marriage partners, and in some cases linked them to psychotic behavior. Such films, Riché suggests, drew on "backlash" formulas of mainstream cinema by imaging Black women as stalkers, edifying class biases that framed such types as pathological in relation to working-class Black women, and concomitantly reinforced longstanding neoconservative ideologies about Black women and Black men. They are valuable to examine in thinking toward a more visionary model of Black love relationships.

Of course, when such defaming images are created of Black women the result is Black men become wary. It's a reasonable reaction. Everyone wants real love and healthy relationships, but apparently, Black women don't know how to have them. Enter Steve Harvey in 2009 with *Act Like a Lady, Think*

Like a Man, which Dale Williams reads critically. A seemingly viable answer acclaimed internationally as the advice women have been asking for,
Steve Harvey's book created controversies mostly due to its antifeminist
message. Dale says to some, Harvey's tactics seemed forced and unrealistic
as he reduced pursuing a man to a strategic plan with antiquated and manipulative tactics, which leaves his female readers no better than he found them.
Yet his advice has been widely received as many still look to Harvey for
answers, but his misogynist point of view ties women to old ideas and traditional ways of thinking by positioning the man in an authoritative role where
he must be pleased, while placing the responsibility of the relationship and
the blame of the decline of Black relationships on African American women.
Dale provides a deeper exploration of the book, ten years later, to determine
if this antifeminist work has any value when exploring the decline of marriage and relationships in the African-American community.

   Growing up in a Christian family in Zimbabwe, I watched and listened to
the rhetoric that women should build their homes. My mother was part of a
women's ministry group that met in each other's homes and sometimes when
they were in our house, I listened. Women admonished each other for dirty
homes, dirty children, and not enough sex. They advised each other with
little tricks on how to keep things interesting and special. They took the sole
responsibility of their marriages upon their shoulders and made it a righteous
thing to be all things for their husbands, children, and church. I was a young
bride, at twenty-one, when I took on the role of sole relationship guardian.
My ex-husband was just three years older and we didn't last long. Domestic
violence, monetary dishonesty, deception, and immaturity were all on my
shoulders. Within two years I was depressed and suicidal. I had moved with
my husband to Canada and had no family close by. We went to a church
where, unlike the church back home, White women stayed out of each other's business. I was completely isolated and felt I had failed. I had tried to be
everything, I worked, I cooked, I cleaned, I maintained a regular sexual
schedule, and I still couldn't make it work. Raised in a church that condemned divorce, I felt stuck. One day, I found myself thinking one of us had
to die for me to be free. I either had to kill myself or kill him. That was the
day I left. I figured, I could recover from divorce, but I could never recover
from taking a life, his or mine.

   Those early impressions of marriage left their mark on my psyche. My
partner is a gentle man, but I still fear that one day I will say something, and
he will hit me. I also fight the temptation to blame myself for everything that
goes wrong between us. I find feelings of guilt rising if we go a few days
without sex. I even find myself resisting the urge to snoop in his phone. Do I
trust him? I do, but I have impressions of *Black men cheat, Black men can't
be faithful, Black men think it's okay to have other women and families
outside their marriage, Black men are abusive, Black men . . . Black men . . .*

Black men. . . . I was raised by a Black man who came home from work at the same time every day and went everywhere else with his wife. When he died, I remember wondering if strange children would turn up at his funeral claiming he was their father even though I knew my father well enough to know it would never happen. It had happened to so many people I went to school with that I took the time to contemplate the possibility.

Karen McMeo focuses on a very crucial and yet neglected aspect of relationship building in "Mental Health and Interpersonal Relationships: A Personal Essay." Her narrative touches at the heart of what we carry into our relationships. The mental impairments we smuggle into our relationships have a significant impact on how we experience love and how we give and receive it. Loving an unhealthy person might seem admirable but as Karen shares, its tantamount to self-destruction. It's even worse when children are born and raised in homes that are pathological.

Relationships are complicated. All couples fight, and all relationships have their tensions. Yet, we should not forget to celebrate the beauty that makes Black love precious. We have cultural differences that I find amusing sometimes. He is from Ghana and I am from Zimbabwe. I admit I have more affinity for his country than he does mine because we had Sally Mugabe, a Ghanaian woman who was the first lady of Zimbabwe when I was a child. Our cuisine is very different, and I have learned to cook a few things that I like. Some dishes smell so strong they fill the space for days and I absolutely hate it! There are times I wish we spoke the same African language, so we can gossip about people in front of them. I enjoy being with an African man. I appreciate that when he travels to Ghana, he brings me a whole suitcase of things that are both new and old to me. So far, I have not experienced anything terribly difficult about our different cultures, maybe because both our families live far away, and we are not subject to extended family drama. I am still learning about his culture, his country, and his character. Just as he is learning mine.

In the last article, "Between an African American and Trinidadian: An Autoethnography of Race, Identity, and Love," Renata Ferdinand provides an intimate look at the social influences that have affected her twelve-year relationship with her husband. She is African American and he is Trinidadian. Amid countless barriers and hurdles, she contends that three important factors have emerged as confounding influences on their relationship, which have led to undue pressure and stress: (1) The American experience of racism and discrimination, (2) the immigrant cultural identity and work ethic, and (3) the mediated and popular cultural images of Black men and women. Renata believes that exploring these factors as they relate to Black relationships will reveal a very complex dynamic and maybe offer a more nuanced way of understanding the subtle, yet treacherous circumstances that lead to failed Black relationships.

The first chapter, "Black Love in the Three Registers" gives the reader some things to contemplate as they encounter the following chapters. This chapter is a psychoanalytic rendition of the very ordinary problems that most couples go through, irrespective of their race. It highlights the ways that couples can grow and address points of conflict. Although it is a hypothetical case, as a therapist, I can attest to these issues in many couples. From counseling countless couples and from my own experiences, I believe that in healthy relationships, the ego must bruise from time to time for the relationship to grow and the relationship must be more important than the things we want from it. Otherwise, we place burdensome expectations from our history on ourselves and our partners.

So, if all couples, regardless of race, experience difficulties, what's so special about Black couples? Black couples deal with signifiers that are given to them by a White supremacist society. We could call these signifiers, stereotypes. Some of them are internalized and used to blind us to the very real and very wonderful people with whom we are in love. This chapter ends in an ambiguous space where the couple can choose to either follow the desires of their egos or the desires of the relationship. It is up to us, Black people, to choose the relationship and the signifiers that will drive our relationship.

Chapter One

Black Love in the Three Registers

Tapo Chimbganda

Black love is an Imaginary object. But it's not just Black love that suffers this ailment; according to Lacan (1953–1954), French psychoanalyst, all love is in the Imaginary because all love seeks to accomplish the same thing, to prop up the ego, to inflate the ego, to protect the ego, and to ingratiate the ego. Love, in other words, exists to please the one *in love.* Lacan believed the human unconscious is structured like a language (Fink, 1997). He reexamined many of Freuds theories and cases, presenting them as objects, conditions, and entries into subjectivity, which culminate into what we regard as psychic experience. One of his more useful theories, in the context of Black love, is the Register theory, which "loosely speaking, the Imaginary, the Symbolic, and the Real can be thought of as the three fundamental dimensions of psychical subjectivity" (Johnstone, 2018). Johnstone explains that Lacan tends to associate (albeit not exclusively) the Imaginary with the restricted spheres of consciousness and self-awareness and it is the register with the closest links to what people experience as nonpsychoanalytic everyday reality. He states that who and what one "imagines" other persons to be, what one thereby "imagines" they mean when communicatively interacting, who and what one "imagines" oneself to be, including from the imagined perspectives of others—are all encompassed under the heading of the Imaginary register (Johnstone, 2018).

Johnstone also says that when he speaks of the Symbolic, Lacan refers to the customs, institutions, laws, mores, norms, practices, rituals, rules, traditions, and so on of cultures and societies. Therefore, individual human beings are born into preexisting language, a preexisting Symbolic order, with preexisting signifiers that will determine many aspects of their lives. Further, Johnstone describes the Symbolic, often referred to as the big Other, as an ideational realm, which when the unconscious, as bound up with that which

9

is Symbolic, is an intricate, labyrinthine web of ideational representations interconnected in multiple sophisticated manners. In other words, the Symbolic is where one experiences the most intimately and subjectively fulfilling social and human connections.

Finally, the Real is the place where one does not want to tarry because according to Johnstone (2018),

> The register of the Real is tricky to encapsulate and evades being pinned down through succinct definitions. Lacan's numerous and shifting pronouncements apropos the Real are themselves partly responsible for this absence of straightforwardness. But rather than being just a barrier to grasping the Real, this absence is itself revelatory of this register. To be more precise, as that which is foreign to Imaginary-Symbolic reality—this reality is the realm containing conscious apprehension, communicable significance, and the like—the Real is intrinsically elusive, resisting by nature capture in the comprehensibly meaningful formulations of concatenations of Imaginary-Symbolic signs. It is, as Lacan stresses again and again, an "impossibility" *vis-à-vis* reality.

Another critical aspect of the Register theory is Lacan's work on *Signifiers*. Signifiers are words that stand in place of an object or desire, thoughts or feelings. Signifiers give meaning to the drama that takes place in the unconscious. In *The Classroom as Privileged Space*, I explain that added to the complexities of the desires that shape blackness, are the signifiers of these desires. "Added to the individual's understanding or awareness of self as a social being is the social reality in which the being must operate" (Chimbganda, 2017, p. 17).

"Black love" is an example of a signifier, which in each of the registers, might signify different things. Ideally, Black love should inhabit the Symbolic register because in this space it can be more giving and outward facing. Other examples of signifiers in this context include *partner* or *spouse*. As a society we assume we know what one means by these words. Hence, even if we do not see or know the person to whom these words refer we assume we know their role in the speaker's life. Signifiers and the objects they represent are not static but unconsciously glide along the axes of desire and relationship. Sometimes #blacklove means something wonderful. Sometimes #blacklove means pain.

Fink (1997) helps us see that "The unconscious is also the Other's discourse in a very straight forward fashion: the unconscious is full of other people's talk, other people's conversations, and other people's goals, aspirations, and fantasies (insofar as they are expressed in words)" (p. 9–10). Thus, the way in which the individual subject, society, and the unconscious relate is through signifiers. While signifiers reveal much to us about the way an individual understands their own history as well as society's interpretation of that individual's history, they can become burdensome in that not all signifiers are desirable or even accurate, for example, stereotypes. Therefore, words such as "black," "white," "Black woman," "White man," as signifiers produced by the social reality in which the people signified by these terms must inhabit and engage as psychic beings. In current sociopolitical discourse, "White man," signifies a person of Caucasian descent who has been propped up by misogyny and white supremacy. In the same vain, when one speaks of a "Black man," the signified figure is one cast in predetermined aggressive and deviant social roles and expectations. To the Black woman, herself signified as unable to give the Black man the love he desires, "Black man" might signify the roving father, the cheating partner, the elusive lover. Clearly, there is a danger of stereotypes becoming signifiers that ruin relationships for Black women and Black men before they even begin.

THE STORY OF TASHA AND JOE

Picture this: A Black woman, Tasha, and a Black man, Joe, swiped right on Tinder. Each saw an attractive face, sexy physique, and endearing smile, all of which in the psychic realm happens in the Imaginary register. They contact each other, chat for a few days in which they pay each other multiple compliments, laugh at each other's quirky jokes, exchange their dreams and aspirations, and finally express they can't wait to meet. Excitedly they set up a first date. The day of the first date, Tasha gets her hair done because she's decided he's worth it. She also gets waxed, not because she puts out on the first date but because it makes her feel more confident to be prepared for any eventuality. "Girl, why on earth does a waxed vagina make you feel confident on a first date?" her friend asks her suspiciously.

Tasha responds with a cheeky smile, "This guy is the one, I can just feel it! I mean he's sweet and charming; never once took things too far; and he has a great job and even talked about travelling to many of the places I like." Her friend's raised eyebrows do not deter her from also wearing her sexiest lingerie underneath her little red dress. Across town in his condo, Joe breaks out his most stylish suit, he plans to take her to a very fancy restaurant, even though his friend advised him, "Bruh, it's only a first date. You don't go all out on a Tinder first date. Ever heard the word: 'catfish?'" But Joe feels something different this time. Tasha understood all his jokes and laughed at them. She is as educated as he is, and her values seem to match his own.

He tells his friends, "It's not like that last date. That girl was so obviously thirsty for marriage and kids. Nah man, this one is special!"

"The foremost Imaginary object is the ego," according to Fink (1997), who explains that the ego is an Imaginary production, a crystallization or sedimentation of images of an individual's own body and of self-images reflected to him or her by others. The object is one toward which libido is directed or withdrawn, as is the case with love objects in Freudian theories (p. 84). So, you see, the brief exchange of ego-driven chat between Tasha and Joe has served the purpose of affirming each other's self-images. It's a great start for any relationship but it's also a slippery slope if they do not move out of the Imaginary into the Symbolic at some point.

The first date goes great, so well, they decide to go dancing after dinner. Tasha loves to dance, and Joe sure knows how to romance a lady on the dance floor. Many dates later, the couple makes love for the first time. For Tasha, it's just as she imagined it would be. Joe is an attentive lover, who puts her needs first. All that talk about Black men not going down on Black women is fake news, she reports to her friend the next day. "Girrrllll, he made my toes and my fingers curl!" She boasts to her friend, who has not had a date in over a year and is seriously thinking of replacing her battery powered boyfriend with a newer model. Likewise, Joe is satisfied with his performance the night before. He is sure he made her come at least three times. And if those noises she made are anything to go by, she will be waiting urgently for their next time.

Three months into the relationship, both Tasha and Joe feel the other is a God-send. The one they prayed for and waited for (not so patiently). Tasha, who is thirty-five years old, is happy she didn't lower her standards and date the delivery guy who spent two months preening like a peacock for her attention. She thinks he was good looking enough, and he spoke to her like a gentleman, but she has always believed it's better to be with a man at least as educated and successful as she is. Her role models, the Obamas, got it right. Tasha is all set to power-couple with Joe. Joe is thirty-eight and decided early in his career as an immigration lawyer to focus on getting to a place where he is a leader not follower. Over the years, he dated several women but none of them seemed to understand why he was so career-focused. Tasha gets it though. She's also career-driven and owns a thriving consultancy. He likes that she owns her own home, is not in debt, and has investment knowledge that has helped her build an enviable portfolio, much better than his own, in fact. They date for several more months before things start to go awry.

Fink (1997) explains that Imaginary relations are not illusory or non-existent relationships, rather they are relations between egos that involve other people whom one considers to be like them for a variety of reasons (p. 84). Thus, an ego-based relationship sooner or later begins to crumble when the elements that one thought signaled compatibility or similarity fade. For Tasha and Joe, it took about seven months for them to start questioning their relationship. Tasha noticed that Joe likes to correct her a lot, like he is making sure she says and does things the way he approves. Joe noticed that Tasha is argumentative. Anytime he helpfully points out her errors, she snaps at him, argues her position, or becomes silent and passive aggressive. She's also started criticizing him a lot. One time, she told him that he wore the wrong shoes with his suit. Yet, at the beginning she always told him she liked his sense of style. He can't remember the last time she complimented him on anything.

Sex has also lost its appeal for both parties. Tasha can't remember the last time she had an orgasm or the last time he gave her oral sex. One time, she is pretty sure he faked it. He was down there making the appropriate noises, but she knows the difference between a tongue and wet fingers. Besides, he kept pressing at her like an elevator button until she finally asked him to stop. That night for the first time in weeks, he chose to leave right afterward. And after several more episodes, where she felt unfulfilled, she stopped faking it. Sex has become a silent affair, where Joe does his thing and she barely participates. Joe feels like Tasha is punishing him for something by just lying there instead of engaging in the love-making with him. She is withholding affection too. And if there is something he cannot not stand, it's a withholding woman. In his opinion, women are supposed to be nurturing and giving. By month eight, both are ready to reactivate their Tinder accounts.

"Girl, I'm so sorry. I really thought you'd found your man," commiserates Tasha's friend.

Tasha sighs, "Me too but he's more interested in himself than he is in me. Do you know at dinner he talked nonstop about some client or case of his? Didn't even ask how my meeting with a potential investor went. I mean, that meeting was a big deal for me!"

In between push-ups and crunches, Joe confides in his friend that he thinks Tasha has lost interest in him because when he was talking about his clash with a racist judge who always turns Black asylum seekers down, she yawned several times and examined her manicure like it was a strange creature. "I mean why do women do that—only like a brother when he is 100 on her? I thought the point of relationships was to have someone to share thoughts, plans, ideas with. Nai-mean?"

His friend shrugs and shakes his head before putting down his dumbbell. "Catfished bruh. I warned your ass. It ain't just fake names and hair. Its fake attitudes and actions too. Women pretend they are into you so you can wine and dine 'em. But it's always all about them. I learned that the hard way, man. Married fifteen years and I have sex twice a year. Valentine's, if I get her something and her birthday, depending on what I get her."

Should Tasha and Joe just break up and seek new horizons on Tinder?

In the Imaginary register, it is difficult to move past hurts and rejections because they are fueled by ego desires. Egocentric relationships tend to be narcissistic and selfish, and cultivate feelings driven by unrealistic ideals and desires. Tasha expected Joe to always make her toes curl and Joe expected Tasha to be a container for all his thoughts and feelings, leaving no room for hers in the relationship. Couples caught in the Imaginary realm, driven by egocentric desires, tend to suffer much more and much longer from mental and emotional fatigue because they are seeking to sustain desires that the partner must fulfill regardless of their partner's own needs. Such ego-based relationships thrive on aggression, alienation, and manipulation. A victim mentality internalizes criticisms and the partner becomes the villain in the story. This can go on for years in some relationships. Fortunately, both Tasha and Joe have a very clear idea about what kind of relationship they want and neither of them are willing to live as a victim.

To elaborate briefly on the Imaginary, referring once more to Johnstone (2018), the Imaginary is necessary or real abstractions, which signals two points: First, as one of Lacan's three basic, essential registers, the Imaginary is an intrinsic, unavoidable dimension of the existences of speaking psychical subjects; one should not try to get rid of it as to do so is like trying to rid oneself of the unconscious—which is neither possible nor desirable. "Second, the fictional abstractions of the Imaginary, far from being merely 'unreal' as ineffective, inconsequential epiphenomena, are integral to and have very concrete effects upon actual, factual human realities." Our relationships must begin and in a fundamental way, even as we become older and wiser, continue to exist (to an extent) within the Imaginary register.

Why? Because the Imaginary is bound up like a (Borromean) knot with both of the other two registers. Johnstone (2018) says, ". . . (Incidentally, the Imaginary and the Symbolic, when taken together as mutually integrated, constitute the field of "reality," itself contrasted with the Real)." According to Lacan, as explained by Johnstone, the Imaginary invariably involves category mistakes. More specifically, it is the register in which the other two registers are mistaken for each other: What is Real is misrecognized as Symbolic (certain meaningless contingent occurrences at the level of the material world of nonhuman objects are viewed as though they were meaningful signs full of deep significance to be deciphered and interpreted). For example, those times when Joe gave Tasha roses, and she spent days with her friend trying to decipher what he meant by it and she came to the hopeful conclusion that it's because he is in love with her even though he hadn't said it and they'd only been dating a couple of months. Thankfully, Tasha's single but albeit wise friend reminded her, sometimes, a guy buys roses because the vendor was especially convincing. They do not signify anything.

On the other hand, "In the Imaginary, what is Symbolic can also be misrecognized as Real," as Johnstone (2018) states, meaning Tasha missed certain signifiers because her ego, in the Imaginary register, didn't like them and erased them. So, she sat in her bed feeling absolutely miserable, and starting to fight a cold because her body was so stressed and fatigued by Joe's inability to communicate in a way that would give her mental relief. Johnstone (2018) expands on this by pointing out that such conversion symptoms are unconscious mental conflicts encoded in language and ideas, suffered as bodily afflictions and ailments.

Back to our lovebirds. . . .

"Hey so I think we need to talk," begins Tasha. Joe resists the foreboding feeling her words trigger for him, but he says nothing, waiting to see where she might go with this talk. "I just feel like lately this relationship has become less pleasure and more hard work. I mean I know it's good to work on one's relationship, but I don't think this is the kind of work I want to be doing."

Joe sighs, he is not sure if he is relieved or disappointed. He chooses to be open in his response, "I hear you and I agree. It's been stressful, and yeah, we need to decide what we are doing. But can we not do it over the phone, please. You can come over. I'll order something and we can talk." He hopes being on his own turf will give him some advantage in whatever transpires. That evening he cleans up an apartment that had become unusually messy and he sets out the flowers he bought and even buys a scented candle like Tasha's been doing for him since they started spending more time together. When she arrives, it is to a sweet smelling and warm space that makes her glad she took this step to fix things.

Joe begins, "I don't know where things went sideways but I want to understand so that I can do better if it's on me to do so." He looks at Tasha, his gaze unwavering, and it reminds her that at the beginning he looked at her like that all the time. Tasha recalls trying to explain his gaze to her high and dry friend, who lately seems more interested in pointing out how much fun Tinder can be. Tasha couldn't find the words then and she can't find the words now, but Joe's gaze is a powerful aphrodisiac for her, and not necessarily in a physical sense. She asks herself if he ever stopped looking at her like that or maybe she stopped noticing.

She smiles at him, "Thank you for being so open, Joe. I want to see if we can work on things too. I mean, we had such a wonderful beginning, it can't just end like this." Joe loves her voice when she smiles. Her voice takes on a quality that draws him to her. It's the first time he realizes that he is in love with her.

These two elements—Joe's gaze and Tasha's smiling voice—that cannot be fully described are in the realm of the Real, where things cannot be symbolized or signified. Couples exposed too much and too long to the Real can start to feel like prisoners to something they cannot identify. Even when they know they need to break up and move on, they remain stuck, unable to extricate themselves from each other. In the Real, love can be experienced as painful, traumatic. Desire is unbearable. Not even the self-seeking ego likes the Real because it can be likened to a badland where everything is potentially destructive. In the Real, the subject is foreclosed, which in psychoanalytic/ clinical terms means psychotic. Words and feelings seem to exist within a dark void from whence meaningful signifiers cannot emerge. To illustrate, think of a psychotic patient, a schizophrenic person who exists in their own world where meanings are different from the rest of society. A schizophrenic person can speak the same words as everybody else, but discourse may be meaningless to the people to whom the words are spoken. Have you ever found yourself questioning your own sanity within a relationship? It is likely you are experiencing it in the Real register. Given enough *un*signified thoughts or feelings, your relationship can become a living hell.

To further help you understand the condition of the Real, think of orgasms. An orgasm is both pleasurable and painful and the longer it goes, the more both these qualities become indistinguishable so that in the end you want it to stop. What words do you use to describe such an experience? For some it is so intense their mind and body instinctively guard against it so that they are not capable of orgasming at all. Some might say the practices of bondage, BDSM (erotic play that includes bondage and discipline; dominance and submission; and other sadistic and masochistic positioning), and other sensation-intense fetishes are a way of prolonging the orgasmic pleasure and pain without suffering the Real quality of it.

Tasha and Joe, thankfully, are not stuck in the Real but like the rest of us experience moments of it that make our relationships a little more mysterious and exciting. They were both disappointed in the last few months of their relationship but that Real something, that both cannot quite explain to their bitter and pessimistic friends causes them to meet up and discuss the situation to see if they can work on getting back on track. They talk at length about their past relationship failures over the Peking duck he ordered from her favorite Chinese takeaway and a bottle of pinot noir. It's the first time they discuss these openly and intimately. They discover patterns that they have maintained in their quest for romance. Joe confesses he has this idea that his woman should be a receptacle for all his thoughts, feelings, and ideas and this makes him neglect hers. Tasha realizes she's somewhat addicted to the first date and that first time high. As time passes, she searches for that same excitement instead of focusing on building a lasting relationship. That night they begin to produce signifiers that do not come from their egos but from the Symbolic realm where the ego is subject to a big Other.

They decide that their big Other—the one who provides signifiers within the Symbolic—should be their relationship, which makes it the Relationship. So, from this point their desires are driven by the Relationship as Other, rather than their egos in the Imaginary. They commit to focusing on communication, being present in the moment, and truly understanding themselves in relation to each other. They decide to let go of expectations of what the other should be or do and focus instead on learning more about each other as individuals.

Lacan's theory teaches us that it is the Other that brings the subject into the Symbolic. The Other can be viewed as authoritative in that it demands of the subject a relationship that is not centered on the ego. In fact, the ego takes a forced vacation, occasionally showing up in those moments, which trigger conflicts but ultimately the relationship is not dictated by Imaginary fantasies. To be clear, what arouses desire in the subject is the Other's desire, not the Other's demand, nor even the Other's desire for this or that particular thing or person (Fink, 1997, p. 91). The function of the Other is to direct the subject's desire but not to cause it. So, while Tasha and Joe might speak of all those qualities they initially fell for, which were in fact about their own egos, in the Symbolic they focus more on the things that build a healthy relationship. Signifiers such as "partner" begin to mean honesty, respect, trustworthy instead of toe-curling and mind-blowing. Not because toe curling and mind-blowing should become a thing of the past, but because the Imaginary and the Symbolic, when taken together as mutually integrated, constitute the field of "reality" (Johnstone, 2018). The reality of most relationships is often ignored in favor of illusionary fantasies. When couples focus on building realistic relationships, a lot of the ego-driven fantasies that would ultimately destroy them are replaced by signifiers that are driven by the Relationship rather than driving the Relationship.

HOW RACIST VIEWS OF BLACK PEOPLE CAN BECOME SIGNIFIERS IN THEIR RELATIONSHIPS

So, if these Imaginary struggles are common to all relationships, why do Black couples appear to struggle so much more than others. Does it mean Black couples never come into the Symbolic or for some reason suffer the Real type of relationship? If Tasha and Joe could make it past their fantasies and egos, why can't other Black couples?

Well, Tasha and Joe were never Facebook kind of people, otherwise they would both currently be displaying "it's complicated" on their profiles. They've been married a little over four years and have two kids, twins born two years into their marriage. Joe has been struggling with the work/life balance and Tasha is trying to sell her business so she can stay at home, at least until the kids are a little more independent. She is both glad and a little jealous that Joe is still working miracles for his immigration clients because it means she can afford to make this decision. As a parent, she does the bulk of the caregiving, but Joe is not an absent father by any means. He never works on weekends and always comes home in time to put the twins to bed. To the outsider they appear to have a solid thing going.

So, what's the problem?

The problem is both of them are Black people trying to build a normal family life without any of the protective factors their white friends have. To sell her business, Tasha has met with several prospective buyers who all question, one way or the other, the accuracy and integrity of the figures she shows them even after they take some time to crunch the numbers themselves. These buyers still express some reservations that to Tasha appear racist. One buyer began the meeting by stating how surprised he was to find she's a Black woman because it's quite an unusual accomplishment that someone from her background would be able to build a thriving business in investments management. The meeting with this man persisted in that tone and Tasha did all she could to remain cool. When she shared the story with her husband he said rather dismissively, "At least they don't think you are trying to bully them. The judge accused me of browbeating him and denied the third appeal by my client today. Why does everything a Black man does have to be interpreted as aggression?" The conversation ends there because the twins are demanding their parents' attention. This happens a lot for Tasha and Joe. They seem to have very little time to finish conversations and it's almost impossible for either one of them to listen to the other and offer some comfort. By the time they are ready for bed, both are irritable and fatigued. And then another day begins.

Joe has also started feeling the pressure of being a sole provider since Tasha stopped working. He worries about everything. Most importantly, if he is spending enough time with his kids. He grew up without a father and wants to make sure his kids never experience the absence of a father. Taking weekends off and coming home early means he is not taking as many clients as he would like. He has a couple of associates that work for him but to him that's added responsibility. One of his associates is a White woman. He hired her straight after her graduation. She's hard working and produces the results he expects but he has heard her on several occasions saying disparaging remarks about her Black clients. When he tried to address it, she cried insisting she is not a racist. Since then he notices she avoids taking on Black clients and also avoids him. He questions the longevity of her career in his firm. The other associate is a Black woman who specializes in spousal immigration. She is also hard working but her behavior toward him is somewhat unprofessional. She constantly crosses boundaries and acts like he is sexually interested in her. He and Tasha have had several arguments about this associate.

It's not that Tasha doesn't trust her husband. It's just that so many Black men cheat. Her mother always told her that and when she was dating, she experienced it for herself. Even her brother tells her it is not natural for a Black man to stay with one woman because slavery altered their relationship DNA, and didn't their African ancestors have many wives? Tasha and Joe hardly have enjoyable sex anymore because having babies caused her to lose some of her sex drive. She is also very tired most days and, to be honest, sex has become more of a chore for her. She finds herself doing it so that he will have no cause to seek it anywhere else. It would seem the couple have drifted back to ego-driven relating and it is taking its toll.

In Black relationships, certain stereotypes that act as signifiers can ruin the prospects of love. Stereotypes that Black men are aggressive, unfaithful, absent, lazy, can take the place of love-affirming signifiers. Black men may find themselves focusing more on proving these stereotypes wrong rather than enjoying their relationships. When stereotypes become signifiers, the tone of the relationship becomes tainted because the Other that is producing these signifiers is not the Relationship but the White Other, which has historically not been just or nurturing to Black people. Black stereotypes are usually in relation to whiteness. The unspoken expectation is that a Black man will cheat, unlike a White man. The unspoken judgment is that Black men are lazy, compared to White men. Therefore, the Black man's relationship becomes subject to whiteness as Other. His motives become proving the Other wrong rather than caring for his partner and children.

Black female stereotypes include angry, overly sexual, argumentative, and worst for Tasha, unable to keep a man. Tasha finds herself unable to express her true feelings in her relationship with Joe. Her best friend is still single and struggling and constantly reminds her that Black women, especially educated and successful Black women can't have good and lasting marriages. Tasha fears that her marriage will end because she's no longer working, has two children, and isn't as fun and sexy as she used to be. She knows that's really what causes her to question his relationship with his associate even though he assures her he maintains professional boundaries and if said associate doesn't change, he will let her go. It doesn't help that when they are in the thick of it, she hears her mother's voice, "No Black man knows how to be faithful. Look at your father! 70 years old and he's still chasing tail like a rabid dog." And her best friend, "Girl, it's worse than the Sahara for people like us. You better hold on to that man like your life depends on it. Coz it does! What'll you do with no business and two bratty kids? So what if he looks elsewhere from time to time? He still comes home to you every night. Besides, your kids need a father more than you need a faithful husband."

Sadly, Tasha suffered postpartum depression after her pregnancy. That and the drastic change in her status, from successful business woman to stay-at-home mother, has been very difficult to cope with. She has no time to seek therapy and feels very isolated. When Joe comes home from work, all she can think is, *I better be at my best because tomorrow morning he goes back to Wanda and Becky and they aren't exhausted, bust-up, Black females with two kids.* By bedtime she feels like an absolute failure because she wasn't her best when the twins made a mess in the dining room. When Joe tried to initiate sex after the kids were in bed she still had some ironing to do.

By the time both Tasha and Joe seek help for their relationship, their mental health has suffered immensely. Like most Black men and women in relationships, Tasha and Joe neglected a fundamental aspect of healthy relationships. How can unhealthy people have healthy relationships? Imagine trying to have a healthy relationship while dealing with a partner who is always irritable, self-loathing, and indecisive. Maybe your partner shows no interest in sex or even going out. Perhaps your partner drinks excessively, or misuses illegal and/or prescription drugs. In some cases, domestic violence follows. It does not matter how much you love your partner or how much you deserve better, unless they seek treatment for their mental health, the chances of your relationship surviving are slim, very slim. It took a lot of insistence for Joe to agree when Tasha suggested it.

"It's a waste of money. What will I learn that I don't already know? That I'm a Black man?" he asks sarcastically?

How I really feel, thought Tasha but instead she says, "Maybe you won't learn anything new but maybe I will, and I need to know how to stay in this relationship with you because we aren't doing well at all, Joe. Remember we promised each other we would honor the Relationship more than our egos?" Joe is not ready to take on more stress and he feels that's exactly what therapy will be. When he finally relents it's because if she asks him one more time, he might say something regrettable. He secretly thinks *this is some White woman shit that she picked up at those play groups she takes the twins to every Friday*. He thinks *those damn groups are full of entitled White women who spend the day doing yoga, getting manicures, and spending money that they don't need to earn because they had children*. When he expresses this the first time, they attend therapy, Tasha is deeply hurt and offended. When they get home, another fight ensues. She accuses him of resenting her for staying home.

"Well yeah, Tasha," Joe bellows over her sobs. "Why you always crying? My mom worked three jobs and still managed to raise all of us. That's what Black women do. I don't get this stay-at-home shit. Don't forget these kids will need more money as they get older."

"But Joe, we agreed we wanted them to enjoy a stress-free childhood as much as possible. If we are both working, they have to get up as early as we do and come home when we do."

"C'mon Tasha, you're trying to live like a White woman with all these expectations. Black women work hard and get shit done. Last week I had to iron my own shirt before work." It's not the first time Joe has said something like this. He also leans on preconceived notions that are detrimental to his marriage. His expectations of his wife are based on his experience of his mother. After his father left them, Joe's mother invested all of her time and energy into raising her children. Although she secretly suffered from depression and constantly struggled with low self-esteem and suicidal thoughts, she did everything for them while avoiding dealing with her own health and well-being but her children did not see it that way, especially Joe. He believes he is successful because his mother sacrificed for him and that's what a good Black woman does. To him signifiers of a Black woman are sacrificial, nurturing, strong, and independent, none of which his wife has achieved in his view. Tasha looks at him and wonders when he looks at her does he actually see her or does he see something else, someone else—just another Black woman, who is failing in her marriage. Despite a rough first session, the couple returns to their therapist. Tasha asks the question that's been on her mind all week. "Joe, when you see me, what do you see? Who do you think I am?"

As you read the essays in this collection, I invite you to analyze for yourself the signifiers that drive Black love. Which signifiers are given by a White supremacist society that is not nurturing of Black love. Also consider, what ego-driven signifiers keep Black couples stuck in fantasies that keep black love from growing and thriving. Finally, consider the Real aspects of Black love, those elements that cannot be signified and yet hold Black couples in psychotic states of love.

REFERENCES

Chimbganda, T. (2017). *The Classroom as Privileged Space: Psychoanalytic Paradigms for Social Justice in Education*. Lanham, MD: Lexington Books.

Fink, B. (1995). *The Lacanian Subject: Between Language and Jouissance*. Princeton, NJ: Princeton University Press.

Johnstone, A. (2018). *Jacques Lacan*. The Stanford Encyclopedia of Philosophy. Edward N. Zalta (ed.). https://plato.stanford.edu/entries/lacan/.

Lacan, J. (1953–1954). *The Seminar. Book I. Freud's Papers on Technique*. Trans. John Forrester. New York: Norton; Cambridge: Cambridge University Press, 1988. p. 142.

Chapter Two

The Black Man's Search for God

Carissa McCray

As Black men search for a quintessential religious identity, the numerous possibilities sometimes create a chaotic voyage of pain, sorrow, and grief with fleeting moments of strength and independence. However, these painful experiences mixed with positive enlightening moments perpetuate an identity that is often misunderstood and ill-conceived creating an unhealthy dynamic in Black relationships. In the search to find God, Black men began developing their own religious foundations to represent their desires and needs that were not and are not found in mainstream religions.

Five-Percent Nation and Nuwaubianism, two religions, which, while promoting this idea of strength and community within Black relationships, perpetuate the idea of misogyny. I believe that the misogynistic nature of Five-Percent Nation and Nuwaubianism stems from the racial and social inequalities that Black men have had to endure. Due to the constant desire and need to have some form of respectable manhood, Black men have created opportunities to overcome and elevate themselves beyond racism, discrimination, and disenfranchisement. However, their efforts to create a strong Black man's identity has led to the destruction of the Black woman's identity.

The following narrative is based on my experiences with and understanding of Nuwaubianism and Five-Percent Nation gleaned from my previous marriage to a member of both religious practices. I share the knowledge I have with others who may have experienced something similar or with those who may feel unable to communicate their experience.

RELIGIOUS BACKGROUND

Throughout my marriage, my ex-husband spent his time searching for God and engaged in researching Islam, Christian, Black Hebrew Israelite, and Nuwaubianism religions. What struck us both as impressive regarding Nuwaubianism was the ability of the leader, Dr. Malachi Z. York, aka Dwight D. York, to create and sustain a Black-owned community in Georgia. Despite several red signs of disheartening information—the government declaring it a cult, lack of paying taxes, and other government findings—Nuwaubianism seemed impressive. Our thinking was that slander and even death can be expected from the same government that illegally tracks its citizens and declares almost every Black movement a hate organization or anti-American.

The idea of a Black-owned community drew me to want to learn more—to study the group as a self-sustaining community. As a researcher, I find that many ideas hold some truth for the overall success and growth of humanity; an idea that we should learn from and discuss issues in constructive discourse for our well-being. However, my thought process was often perceived as a green light by my ex-husband who proceeded, with self-righteous justification and the "Right Knowledge" of Nuwaubianism to lead our family destructively.

Nuwaubianism is a mixture of Christianity, Islam, Judaism, Kemetism, Five-Percent Nation, and extraterrestrial religions that place Black people as supreme beings and White people as the devil. This idea was not only grounded in ancient religious practices but highlighted in how the Bible was used as a tool to enslave Black people. Beginning his teachings in the late '60s and gaining popularity through the '80s, York capitalized on the discrimination and violence toward Black people at the hands of White Americans who were pastors and priests, everyday citizens, and political leaders. The idea that Black people did not have to wait to die and go to heaven for peace, that they can have their *own awakening* right here and right now, delivered a positive and strong message to many Black people across Brooklyn, Harlem, DC, Baltimore, and Trinidad accounting for thousands of members before 1980.

Before becoming heavily involved in the Nuwaubian Nation, my ex-husband became a member of the Five-Percent Nation. Like York and his creation of Nuwaubian Nation, the Five-Percent Nation began in New York City founded by Clarence Edward Smith, aka Clarence 13X, aka, Allah the Father. After leaving the Nation of Islam, Smith's organization appropriated some aspects from the Nation of Islam, proclaimed that White men were the devil, and asserted that Black men were gods. The name Five-Percent Nation derived from Smith's concept that 85 percent of the world are controlled by the government, that 10 percent of the world were aware of the truth, and that 5 percent knew the truth and were missioned to teach it to others. Smith, as the leader of the Five-Percent Nation, sought to maintain Black communities by any means necessary, which included both conflict and cooperation with White politicians and business owners. Following his assassination, Smith's teachings have been open to interpretation by many of its followers whose choices reflect both positively and negatively for the Five-Percent Nation.

Both York and Smith became father figures for my ex-husband. He worshipped them and felt that he could gain some form of manhood if he was respected and praised as a god. My ex-husband began to feel that people should be blessed that he was in their presence because he was a god able to give them "Right Knowledge" and awaken them from their intellectual slumber. As he learned more about the two religions, he began to piece both forms of religion together to create his own identity as a god. However, because the Five-Percent Nation proclaimed Black men as gods with their own ability to establish and maintain their religious divinity, my ex-husband gravitated heavily toward Nuwaubianism.

With time and through interactions with other believers and followers of these religions I learned that as religions, neither Nuwaubianism nor Five-Percent Nation are immune to the negativity that arise from ideological practices ranging from oppressive cleansing of human beings, molesting children, and financial insidiousness. Like other religions, the actions of the leaders and patrons do not stand as indicative of the entire religious organization. Here, I highlight the imperative to understand how the idolizing of religious leaders might lead to neglecting the primary purpose of a religious organization. This information is based on my experience and accounts I gathered from other disenfranchised and alienated Black people who left the religions because it was no longer meeting their needs.

Child Molestation: In 2004, York, convicted of child molestation and racketeering, was sentenced to 135 years in a supermax prison after over ten years of FBI investigation. This conviction was not York's initial confrontation with law enforcement. In 1988, York was convicted of obtaining a birth certificate with a falsified birth certificate. In 1993, after receiving anonymous letters informing of his misconduct, the FBI began its formal investigation into York and the Nuwaubian compound in Georgia. The initial investigation from the FBI was due to the religion's purported aggressive approaches to overthrow the government in Putnam County; allegations of arson, welfare fraud, and extortion.

Concerned members, beginning in the 1990s, began to document their time within the Nuwaubian religion and the compound as that of a cult. Women reported how they were separated from their husbands and children even though York preached and taught the need of nuclear families. Additionally, the FBI began receiving anonymous tips of child molestation and sexual abuse. Due to the separation of mothers, fathers, and children, York had easy access to children with or without parental knowledge. York, positioned as a leader and god, had brainwashed the minds of vulnerable members including children who did not speak out due to fear and/or respect. Members were also separated from their family and friends who did not belong to the Nuwaubian Nation. Therefore, distrustful members were unable to leave without abandoning their loved ones. The teachings of York were so ingrained that members are still proclaiming York's innocence regarding the molestation counts.

Violence against Women and Misogyny: Smith's original teachings were traditionally based on patriarchal adoption of harsh misogynistic practices that are still reflective in the organization today. Although, it is important to note that the Five-Percent Nation began its religious beliefs with men and women being closely related in terms of equality. Men were gods and women were earths that made it possible for gods to sustain existence through nurturing; however, the choice to be equal was left up to individuals. The original teachings by Smith asserted that because God was in all things, that included women as well. The implication of this thinking was that men and women should be treated with equality because the balance of the world depends on the balance of masculine and feminine energies. In the Five-Percent Nation, a woman has her own divine right; yet, depending on the doctrine adopted by the man in her life—father, brother, or husband—she could not free one's self and obtain her own divinity. Misogynistic practices included: remaining silent while men are speaking; backlash when attempting to become educated outside of the Nation; refraining from birth control so men could have as many children as possible; polygamy and/or serial monogamy; arranged marriages; and forcing traditional female roles of mother and housekeeper.

BLACK-BASED RELIGION AND BLACK MEN

Black men entering and remaining in religions such as Nuwaubianism or Five-Percent Nation are looking for the possibility to be men, to protect their women or partners, home, and children. As a community, we are aware that men need to be able to provide and protect to feel as if they can have successful relationships. These religions provide that opportunity for the Black man to feel he has regained his manhood. However, I watched my ex-husband's manhood rise through the detriment of those around him.

In my experience, those who believe in Nuwaubian or the Five-Percent Nation, and almost every religion, are searching for power. This search does not begin as power over others but rather power over self and the ability to make one's own decisions and circumstances. Manhood, defined as the need to protect and provide for loved ones, has been consistently and systematically stripped from Black men for most of their American history. During slavery, Black men could do little to nothing as they watched their women and children raped, beaten, and/or sold. During the Reconstruction period, Black men were sharecroppers who struggled to get out of debt, feed their families, and provide for their children. And, during Reconstruction, Black men established communities and held official positions in federal, state, and local government, which were then dismantled due to Jim Crow and *Plessy v. Ferguson*'s proclamation of separate but equal. The problem of separate but equal was not the separation but the discrimination, unfair practices, and inequality that developed and grew substantially. Post-Reconstruction, the Black man was in a difficult situation. Media, interactions with White men and women, segregation, and other varied, yet dehumanizing experiences created a new type of Black man that is still perpetuated throughout society. That Black man, created by the post-Reconstruction era, was deemed lazy, violent, and uneducated with dangerous virility that should evoke fear. As modern history unfolds, these images still exist.

Religion did not change while Black men leaving slavery and attempting to build a life for themselves and their loved ones faced oppression. In fact, the Bible was the device used by Christian stakeholders to justify the enslavement of those with darker skin because "Cain was marked with dark skin as his punishment for killing Abel," and his descendants carried the mark as well. The continuation of slavery was justified with verses such as Colossians 3:22: *Servants, obey in all things your masters according to the flesh;* Ephesians 6:5: *Servants, be obedient to them that are your masters according to the flesh, with fear and trembling.* Other verses were used to perpetuate the myth of slavery being acceptable for Christians to allow. Post-slavery, the Bible, used by both Black and White Christians, ensured Black people remained complacent within their circumstances because God requires patience and humility. For example, Galatians 6:9: *Let us not become weary in doing good, for at the proper time we will reap a harvest if we do not give up;* 2 Corinthians 4:17: *For our light and momentary troubles are achieving for us an eternal glory that far outweighs them all;* Romans 5:3: *Not only so, but we also glory in our sufferings, because we know that suffering produces perseverance.*

Dissenters of Christianity believe the Bible was not written for the Black man to be successful, therefore they must create their own religions that would ensure that Black men where empowered and could regain their manhood rather than remain enslaved by dogmatic religious ideology that placed Black men as the least desirable of human beings. In creating and following these pro-Black religions in the 1960s and 1970s, they were rejecting the God who endorses the slavery and suffering of those of dark skin. These religions have been sustained, despite their negative impact to Black families, communities, and self, through the continued use of the Bible to justify wrongdoing. We see it even in the present justification of government misconduct: Romans 13:1–2, *Obey the government, for God is the One who has put it there. There is no government anywhere that God has not placed in power. So those who refuse to obey the law of the land are refusing to obey God, and punishment will follow.*

MY EX-HUSBAND, THE GOD OF HIMSELF.

During my marriage, I kept a journal—a practice I began as a child and continue to this day. Sometimes, I go back to those old journals to reflect and provide myself with reasons for why I should take an attitude of gratitude. Below is an excerpt from a journal I kept from 2011. At the time of writing, I was two years into my marriage and my daughter was two years old.

> *Everyday it's the same thing: I wake up, get dressed, drop her off at daycare, go to work, pick her up, come home to a messy house and the person I chose to be my husband because of the potential I saw in him is still in pajamas with no prospect of a job.*
> *This is tiring, and I don't know what else to do about it. He stays on the internet researching Nuwaubian ideas rather than work. Every day, he's talking about how he's filled with "Right Knowledge" and I'm not living up to the role of a wife. I ask him when he's going to work: "I'm not working a White man's job." I try to encourage him with suggestions for becoming a self-made man, but he needs money first. Without money, what is he going to "invent," how are we going to survive?*
> *I've even tried talking to his mother. She's in denial about her son. I ask her to convince him to work at McDonald's or somewhere. She says her son is too smart to be in a place like that. But he needs a job.*

At this point in my marriage, my husband was fully but in parts a believer of the Five-Percent Nation, Nation of Islam, and Nuwaubian Nation. He thought himself god and felt that so many things were beneath him. He felt that White men were the devil and there was no need to communicate with them about anything, let alone work with them.

I began to sink and struggle. My desire to obtain further education was demeaned anti-Black because that meant I wanted to be like White people. Working as a teacher and collaborating with White teachers meant I wanted to be like White people. Asking my husband to get a job where a White person worked meant I wanted to be with a White man. The historical animosity, hurt, betrayal, and subjugation of Black men by White men fueled my ex-husband's desire to have a deity representative of his *self*. The initially justifiable dislike and distrust of White men became an obsessive hatred that haunted our relationship. Because God is supposed to be all-powerful; all-knowing and sovereign unto himself, my ex-husband became his own god and decided he had control over diverse circumstances, especially his own life. However, in doing so, he perpetuated the ideas that other religions possessed—control and subjugation of others.

Every day in my home, the White man was a topic of discussion because someone had to be blamed for poor decisions and outcomes. My home became a home of many gods but the god that dominated our lives and controlled our actions and decisions was the White man. Seeking to understand what drove my ex-husband to embrace Black-based religions and obsess over the White man's oppressive behavior to the point of becoming stagnant was difficult. I did not have time to be his therapist; I was taking care of a home and raising our daughter. However, I had to know. I understood that knowledge, discussion, and reflection of our past and present lives can destroy generational curses and allow our lineage to live better than we were able.

I knew my ex-husband had an absent father. That was one of the things that initially connected us. He wanted to be a better husband and father than his father. However, due to the lack of discussion and acknowledgment of the hurt and animosity he had for his father, a new malefactor had to exist—the White man. It seems that as a Black man, recognizing that another Black man—one's father—hurt them is too taboo to discuss and makes one seem weak. There are many possible reasons for the lack of acknowledging fatherly hurt. Some stem from the fear of admitting that the closest person to them was detrimental to their development. Additionally, as an adult attempting to acknowledge and rectify the hurt and pain from one's father, a man must admit that he is still hurting, which does not support the ideals of manhood. Lastly, the anger Black men have for their father continues because as current fathers, they must forgive themselves to move forward by forgiving others. All these factors were a rich recipe for the toxic masculinity that inhabited my home.

My ex-husband knew his grandparents—both maternal grandparents and his paternal grandmother. I know both my maternal and paternal grandmothers. However, we both were searching for more familial ties within our lineal history. Being part of Nuwaubianism and Five-Percenters, my ex-husband was able to reclaim his own greatness, fight against racial discrimination and equality, and have a self-determined purpose rather than live his life for someone else but, the driving force behind these religions did not address or discuss the hurt, depression, and anger that came from not knowing his father and his roots. The religion did not account for the aperture that motivated his decisions; it plastered over the search for that most crucial answer to the question: Who am I?

Many of us, Black people, struggle with who we are because we do not know where we come from. Our histories are clouded and tainted with no one willing to discuss the hidden or forgotten; therefore, our degrative cycles continue. As these Black-based religions created their own narrative, they provided Black men with the ability to escape their negative and traumatic pasts while emphasizing that they were gods whose responsibility it was to lead the lost and troubled sheep into an empowered future. The Black man becomes the savior that he desired for himself, the family man he desires to be, and the continuation of a bloodline manifested in greatness, godliness, and reverence.

My ex-husband tried to completely distance himself from White men by rejecting not just Christianity but also employment, education, and anything else he perceived as representative of whiteness. The more he struggled to be a god unto himself, the more the animosity and fear of White men as the devil grew and negatively consumed him. When the expectations and changes he sought in his fatherly relationships with Black religious leaders and their religious ideology of the Black man as god, did not manifest, he fell deeper into the abyss of depression. In one of my journal entries during my marriage, I reflected on how several circumstances contributed to the possible depression of my ex-husband and the serious breakdown of our relationship.

> *I think he suffers from depression. And I think it stems from his childhood and these religions that allow him to misdirect his aggression toward women. But I feel like that is an excuse because many people have become successful from their horrible conditions.*
>
> *All he talks about is his father. One minute he hates him, the next he admires him. I think the lack of reconciliation and communication about his past is causing more problems than I can allow to influence me. I have to think about my mental health too.*
>
> *He still doesn't have a job. The White man is still to blame—oppression. His mother is to blame—she doesn't do enough to support him. I'm to blame— I have a Master's degree and I make more money. Our daughter is to blame— he has to take care of her. My miscarriage is to blame—he lost his chance for his first child to be a son. Not only his first child son, but according to Nuwaubianism, his "Sun," "God," "Lineage."*
>
> *All he does is drink and let everyone know how they contribute to his horrible circumstances. He says he isn't drinking, but I can smell it on him and I've seen pints hidden in the back of cabinets, under the beds, and in the toilet tank.*
>
> *I've recommended counseling. We've gone a couple times. He's combative and the counselor recommended he find someone for himself. He thinks himself a god, but has failed at so many things. I'm sure this is taking a toll on him. For how can he believe himself all powerful when he can't even be sober for 24 hours?*

As seen above, the toll of Black men struggling to find themselves via religion can lead to an insurmountable idea of perfection. At a moment of failure, my ex-husband did not blame himself and reflect. Instead, he lashed out at those around him with an emphasis on the women in his life, even his daughter. This self-destructive behavior manifested in alcohol or drug addiction, emotional, physical, and/or verbal abuse, or a deepening inferiority complex. There are numerous reasons why women stay, for me, my self-esteem was so low that some attention was better than no attention. I also suffered from shame. I knew I should not have married; however, I wanted to prove something to those around me. In turn, I was ashamed to leave or to express the magnitude of how corrupted my ex-husband had become due to his father issues, White-man issues, and belief systems. In various discussions with women who have dealt with abusive relationships because of their brother's, father's, or husband's act of self-proclaiming himself as god, women considered their low self-esteem, shame, and feeling they had no one with whom they could confide.

A SISTERHOOD OF HURT

Speaking with other women, their stories sound like mine. One woman, permitted me the opportunity to read, copy, and include a portion of her journal.

> *After being first separated and then pending divorce from my husband for several years, I was ready to remarry my love. But the church would not remarry me because I was not a widow. Well, I might as well have been because my first husband died from being "a Black man on planet earth." As an American Black man, he took all the poisons and then exhibited all the signs and symptoms.*
>
> *See, I was clueless to most of the poisons being from the Caribbean. I met him when he was 15 years old (pretending to be 18 years) and he was already angry—I saw it as strength and the outcome of being raised by a single Black woman who had been hurt and turned bitter from poverty. I attempted to introduce him to God, but the only God he wanted was one who would be his father. First, it was the 5% [Five-Percent Nation] where Black men in urban New York City told themselves they were gods. Yet, they still were not driven for life, acted a fool, and filled the penal systems instead of universities.*
>
> *Because of his need to have a father figure, his drive toward different forms of religion were based on the men he worked with or the men who provided him with some form of employment, nurturing, or mentorship. This meant that whenever he disagreed or felt neglected by the men in his life or quit or was fired from a job his religious values swayed as well. Eventually, he settled on Nuwaubianism because he felt that he could justify whatever choices he made: infidelity, multiple children by multiple women, women staying at home and collecting welfare, back-to-back pregnancies, homeschooling, disregard to post-secondary education, and other forms of keeping women subjugated on the virtues and ethics of the religion.*
>
> *The thing I hate most about his search for religion is that it nurtured the anger in my sons and busted my spirit. My sons are not only searching for a father, they are angry, engaged in self-destructive behaviors like drugs and*

alcohol, and attempt to use the tenants of their father's religions to abuse their authority in their relationships—personal and professional.

One of the major, and saddening, ramifications of the Black man's search for God through Nuwaubianism and the Five-Percent Nation, is the inner turmoil that is not addressed, rather exacerbated. As a god, a Black man failing at any aspect in his life warrants some form of justification. Someone must be responsible for the lack of income, lack of job, lack of fathering. Even though the White man was the one blamed, even though the father was the one culpable for the initial inception of pain, the wife, mother, or daughter becomes the scapegoat. She is an easy target because she is there. There is expediency in being able to express one's animosity, fear, pain, and suffering through the subjugation of others. The role of the woman in the relationships and marriages where the man is feeling continuously and habitually oppressed will result in her oppression.

The women in the family become casualties of their relationships because of poor paternal relationships and misguided attempts at manhood. The trauma of fatherlessness and foreclosed manhood is not discussed. The mental strain of the struggle to be a man is not addressed. As Black boys, there is no father to provide support and demonstrate grit and resilience in the face of struggle. When these men enter relationships with women, their agony, skepticism, injury, hostility, and bitterness become aggression that manifests in domestic and family violence. But the anger is not only contained in the family home, it spills out onto coworkers, service providers, and general society causing the man to isolate within his haven—his home—where he is omnipotent.

I witnessed within my ex-husband a euphoric intoxication from transferring the pain and suffering to someone else. When he was in pain, causing me pain removed or alleviated, even momentarily, the agony. Rather than rectify the emotions related to his father, like other Black men, he continued the negative cyclical behavior that caused the initial hurt and pain. A general lack of communication between us occurred, and, possibly due to the broken idea of manhood, he showed no emotional weakness. Anger became the only permissible emotion between us.

The wife, sister, or mother of a broken man becomes his scapegoat because fear, animosity, and obsession with White men caused her husband, father, or brother to be silenced. Historically, Black men were forced into silence using diverse methods of physical or mental abuse by White men. When speaking out for those they loved, Black men risked lynching, beatings, dismissal from jobs, or worse. Now, the silence occurs almost innately. Black men, even with religions that bolster them as gods, see White men, the same men they hate yet fear, as gatekeepers. Because of this silenced fear and animosity toward White men, Black men take these feelings home. Rather than discuss and/or rectify their relationship with White men, Black men bring those emotions home to their mothers, wives, and children. Sadly, due to the perceived recrimination in the eyes of their mothers, wives and children for the failure to live up to their ideological manhood these men erect towers of discipline, religiosity, and purity that further alienate them from the only people who are actually there for them.

I remember coming home one day from work and another woman and her small son were in our home. My ex-husband had picked our daughter up from daycare and cooked dinner. I told him my daughter and I were leaving to let him figure out his life. His response was that because he was Nuwaubian, he can have multiple women and he was going to adopt this woman's child as his own. I left with my daughter and went to the ATM to have cash-at-hand. However, my account was in deficit by $300. When I called the bank, they notified me that my ex-husband had taken almost $1,000 out of the account and since they were joint accounts, my permission was not needed. Upon calling my ex-husband, he told me that as a god anything I earned belonged to his household. I was forced to stay with my aunt that night and many other nights due to my ex-husband taking my car, household property, and more money. His verbal and emotional abuse toward me was justified by his self-proclaimed deity—he was a god and god can say what he likes. As a woman, I knew better than to allow this to happen. As an educated woman, I knew I had options. Until I could no longer justify my suffering and that of my daughter, I stayed and attempted to heal a man whose problems were bigger than I was and still bigger than I am.

CONCLUSION

The relationships that are forged in our childhoods have an impact on us as adults. The impact can either be positive or negative depending on how we have reconciled those past traumas through acknowledgment, reflection, forgiveness, and our commitment to develop and sustain positive change. Black fathers are key figures in the development and manifestation of their sons' experiences in future relationships. Due to anger and animosity, Black men have created religions that reflect both the traumas of society and the traumas of their lives. Even though religions such as Nuwaubianism and the Five-Percent Nation begin on a premise to uplift the Black community, the leaders of these religions take on the role as father causing the followers to idealize the leaders as impervious to flaws. This idea is manifested in Black male relationships. If questioned or if expectations are not met, Black men are unable to deal with their imperfections and produce destructive behaviors toward themselves and others. As Black men attempt to build positive mental health, the search for God should not be attached to the search for a perfect

Black father. Healing from with one's past trauma should aid in improving the lives of Black men so they can seek to fulfill their own perspective of manhood rather than the religious perspectives that perpetuate negative emotional trauma.

FURTHER READING

Dorman, J. (2013). *Chosen People: The Rise of American Black Israelite Religion.* New York: Oxford University Press.
Hughley, E. (1982). *The Truth about Black Biblical Hebrew-Israelites (Jews): The World's Best Kept Secret.* Hughley Publishers.
Palmer, S. (2016). *The Nuwaubian Nation: Black Spirituality and State Control.* New York: Routledge.

Chapter Three

Black British Women, Love, and the Politics of Choice

Jade Benn

In this piece, I seek to explore the intricacies of our choosing in the context of romantic relationships, using my relationship with Jamal as the case in point. Black, professional (and semiprofessional) British women, originally from working-class backgrounds (or otherwise) enjoy a degree of agency in the decisions they make romantically, however, the purpose of this essay is to explore the ways that sociological, economic, and psychological factors impact this degree of agency. I seek to make this piece relatable, entertaining, and analytical with the intention of fulfilling a host of important intentions. These include shedding light on the issues that affect a specific demographic in a Western context as we witness Black women becoming among the most educated minority ethnic women in Western societies, while simultaneously grappling with common sociological, economic, and psychological issues that consequently complicate the choices we make. I also write this for my own validation and redemption—writing this essay has helped me to understand and accept what I have ultimately grown through. I intend for this endeavor to go some way in assisting young professional Black women as they endow themselves with an awareness of who they are while navigating love and choosing romantic partners. Lastly, I want to affirm readers by informing them that they deserve the love that they are conditioned into ascribing to visible White structures.

This piece will explore both mine and Jamal's starting points, which fundamentally informed our choices and behaviors while providing context. It will explore the sociological, psychological, economic, and political realities that influence the choices women like me may make, and the reasons why we may date and pursue men like Jamal. This will include the impact of interracial dating, self-esteem, and the unequal playing field Black girls start on, the changing status of Black British men and women, and lastly, the inevitable commonalities and attraction informed by common and proximate socialization.

CAN *YOU* MELT MY LOINS?

In all honesty, I was never blown away by Jamal. We never had any real passions in common and although he is an attractive man, he was never able to exactly "melt my loins," so to speak. I made what I thought were rational decisions when it came to choosing him as a partner based on commonalities and attraction that went beyond the physical. Existing in certain spaces as a Black working-class woman brings about a heavy feeling of imposter syndrome and an inevitable lack of confidence. Specific to me, I am teasingly called "ghetto" and "yardie"[1] by friends and associates. The generally serious expression I unconsciously wear on my face is often described as "rude" or "scary," albeit in jest or in an attempt to break some perceived ice. The way I dress, wear my natural hair, sport long nails, and my figure garner anything from jokes among friends about how "Black" and/or "ghetto" I come across, to comments made by supervisors and managers about "the way my clothes fit my figure compared to other members of staff." Although generally comfortable to be me and live with the elements of myself that are described as "Black," "ghetto," "intimidating," and "scary," entering predominantly White patriarchal spaces such as the Academy brought anxieties with it that were directly connected to feelings of not belonging and not being refined enough. When considering love, the thought of qualifying as a love interest to someone who is aesthetically or stylistically better suited to be comfortably placed in White spaces (whether a Black, Asian, or White man), fills me with discomfort and admittedly, distaste. I question how I will be perceived, if I'd be valued, and how I could possibly be understood.

What attracted me to Jamal was a perceived common affinity based on identities we had carved out for ourselves informed by race and class, and where (geographically) we were socialized for most of our lives. Though Jamal chose to exist in a more extreme space in the working-class underbelly within which we both grew up, there were commonalities I found comforting and within which I felt understood. Jamal and I lived in inner-city London, went to school in the city, and were socialized among other inner-city second and third-generation kids. We ate the same foods, listened to the same music, and frequented similar places for socializing and entertainment. We heard the same gossip, understood and spoke the same slang, and in some areas of our lives shared the same groups of associates. We could go to an old friend's birthday and be comfortable because there'd be people we both knew in attendance. There were many unspoken mantras we both respected and up-held that we understood culturally, like believing in God or not using drugs. We measured ourselves with a similar yardstick in the sense that our desire to succeed and be better as people holistically came from a similar desperation and affinity to change the realities of those we loved. Our aspirations looked similar also—to be able to buy a home, a new car, provide comfortably for a small family, travel once a year—simple, arguably mediocre, but reflective of the in-common lack we'd experienced.

Gratefully, I felt like Jamal almost rebelliously appreciated my beauty and held it in high esteem in the context of a wider society that did not. As a dark-skinned woman, there are undeniably fewer places to be seen and ad-mired in Western media, television, film, fashion, beauty, and social media. The influences of white supremist ideals posited daily inherent experiences of rejection and exclusion for me as a dark-skinned Black woman. Many times, I appreciated acknowledgments such as "you are pretty for a dark-skinned girl" or being the subject of other Black girls' hair envy, or being described as looking like I had a "mix." However, for the most part the object of Black men's desires were overwhelmingly women who looked very dif-ferent from me, and so Jamal's appreciation of dark-skinned women general-ly was noble. What compounded the significance of my desirability in Ja-mal's eyes was the fact that he was lighter than me, conventionally attractive, and would be acknowledged as attractive by a plethora of women from different backgrounds. So, there was even a degree of misplaced gratitude attached to Jamal's ability to "see" me and love me.

Jamal was attractive and equally desirable to me because he understood me, saw me, and accepted me. As I write and think about what fueled some of my feelings toward Jamal, I feel sad coming to terms with the fact that I essentially felt misplaced and misunderstood by wider society, almost des-perately finding a place in Jamal and men like him where I finally felt attractive, appreciated, and accepted.

BLACK BRITISH PEOPLE AND MODERN DATING

The marriage of Prince Harry and Meghan Markle brought the topic of interracial dating into public discourse in a more nuanced manner and so previously sparse statistical focus has been redirected to White men dating Black women. Prior to this, Black men, particularly those well-educated or professionally successful, dating White women were (and still are) a very normalized phenomenon. In 1996, the *Independent* reported "40 per cent of young Black men in Britain are married to, or live with a White partner." In the same year, interracial dating between Black women and White men was far less common with around 20 percent of Black women having a White partner (Barker, 1996). In 2009, almost fifteen years later, Song reported that interracial marriages were on the rise in the USA but remained most prominent as a phenomenon in Europe, especially among Black and White people; with about half (50%) of British-born Black men living with a White woman. Statistically, on a macroscale and on a microscale, as per my own experiences (and the experiences of Black women around me), the pool appears to be somewhat limited when it comes to finding Black men socially and economically suited to young Black British women on the rise.

In this age, finding romance via dating apps is an increasingly popular way for young working people to embark on love and dating. Unfortunately, this vastly growing arena is one that excludes Black women specifically. OKCupid published data in 2014 which revealed that Black women received the least messages on dating app platforms and the least responses to their "likes" (Petter, 2018). Similarly, *Inverse* and *Quartz* published data on the desirability of Black women and Asian men finding that both groups were least desirable to the opposite sex across all ethnic groups, with White men and Asian and Latin women reported as most desirable to the opposite sex across all ethnic groups (Francisco, 2017).

As explored by Ralph Richard Banks (2011) in *Is Marriage for White People?,* I want to look at the socioeconomic status of Black men and how this causes a depreciation of the quality of Black men and a constriction of the dating market. In Banks's chapter on the man shortage, he explores how Black male incarceration specifically restricts the markets for poorer, working-class Black women, and how worsening economic prospects for Black men inevitably position them in different social strata's than Black women, whose economic prospects have and continue to improve. Though Banks comments on the US context, commonalities hold and ring true to the British context.

Although less extreme than the situation in the United States, Black men are grossly overrepresented in all areas of the UK criminal justice system (in arrests, prosecutions, convictions, and the prison population). According to the 2011 Census, 86 percent of the UK was White while 3.3 percent of the population considered itself Black (Caribbean or African), but the arrest rate per 1,000 of the population in 2016 reported that 47 per 1,000 Black people were arrested compared to 13 per 1,000 in the case of White Brits, meaning a Black Brit is three times more likely to be arrested. Similarly, among the prison population, Black people are grossly overrepresented—12 percent of the population is Black; in real terms this translates to 47 per 10,000 Black British prisoners compared to 15 per 10,000 White British prisoners. To convey the bleakness of the picture further, Black people had the highest reoffending rate of all ethnic groups, with 34 percent of Black offenders committing a proven reoffence within one year. On average a Black offender committed 3.52 reoffences in their lifetime, and served the highest percentage of their sentence lengths compared to all other ethnic groups, suggesting that the time Black people spend in the criminal justice system is significantly lengthy once an initial offence was convicted and prosecuted (National Statistics, 2017).

Educational attainment has worsened for Black boys compared to their female counterparts at secondary school, however, further and higher educational statistics differentiating gender were unavailable for review here. During secondary school, Black girls did better by an average margin of 12 percent to Black boys in 2015/2016, and Black boys had the lowest educational attainment at the end of secondary school among all boys in the UK (Department for Education, 2017). We can assume more Black girls are attending university by looking at the national picture, which reports that significantly more British girls attended university from 2012 to 2017, with the statistics on Black male professional employment corroborating this assumption as eleven of London's top graduate employers recruited a total of 1803 graduates in 2016, however only thirty of these recruits were Black men (HESA, 2018; Hunte, 2017).

Black British women therefore find themselves dating and embarking on relationships with Black men whose prospects and life experiences will inevitably look very different to theirs. This was my reality with Jamal. I look back now and understand that Jamal was truly an extreme case, however, in being with him I did myself a disservice in many ways which I only came to realize when I landed a job which necessitated a full police check. Using my better judgment, I did not list any relationship with Jamal on the form, but that decision caused me to think—in my mind I intended to marry Jamal, but this form revealed the real implications of such a decision.

Less time and greater accessibility via our smartphones and social media mean dating apps are a far more likely go-to for professional and semi-professional working men and women looking to meet people. I would argue that the pool of Black men on dating apps does not generally include men like Jamal who exist on the fringes of mainstream society. Men like Jamal place less emphasis on the online world for reasons rooted in paranoia (for example, Jamal often concealed his identity on the limited social media platforms he used, expressing that he felt like social media was used as a tool by law enforcement agencies to collect data and build criminal cases; and by his "enemies" seeking information for insidious reasons). Black men like Jamal at times also logistically lack access to the internet because of the unstable and haphazard nature of their lives—a fixed abode with steady Wi-Fi or a mobile phone contract for a smartphone with enough data allowance are not normalized luxuries for many of these men.

In my experience, men like Jamal are more likely to meet women they have some background knowledge of, either because the female went to a local school or shares acquaintances, which therefore provides a degree of security that satisfies the suspicious way these men view women and the world more generally. Jamal knew me from thirteen years old because we had mutual friends. Remembering me at a friends' eighteenth birthday party we both attended, Jamal went on to ask around about me instead of independently getting to know me, which further demonstrates his lack of trust in the subject of his romantic interests. In the same way that Jamal exhibited paranoia and a lack of trust in other areas of his life, his approach in love and forming relationships was not dissimilar, and therefore the idea of speaking to and then meeting someone completely unknown and trusting them to be honest about who they are doesn't seem like an appealing way to meet women for men like Jamal. Coupled with isolation and a perceived lack of interest on platforms like dating apps and social media, the chances afforded to men like Jamal to date Black women, are magnified.

SHEER LUCK

I was raised in a single-parent home in inner-city London by a mother who was also raised by a single woman in the inner-city. Both my mothers and grandmothers trajectory within the context of intimate and romantic relationships were significantly traumatic. Both suffered different forms of abuse from Black men who suffered some form of addiction. My mum watched her uncle physically throw my grandfather out of the family home after breaking a chair over my granny's back, and thereafter, didn't witness my granny have any more intimate or romantic relationships. Similarly, after the death of my stepdad in 2005, I have not witnessed my mum having a stable, committed, traditionally monogamous romantic relationship.[2]

Fatherlessness created an inescapable void in my core during my formative years, so my relationship with *my*self in relation to men would always be inevitably unhealthy, if not acknowledged, and worked on. My father was a long-term heavy drug user and I now understand his addictions and toxic narcissism informed how he would continually treat my mum and me. Before I had the chance to acquire the range and agency necessary to understand my father, our, albeit limited, interactions bred feelings of rejection and an innate perception of undesirability, inextricably linked to how men in future romantic encounters would predictably see me. Before I had the opportunity to establish a healthy or positive self-perception, my self-esteem had taken a battering. In tandem with these realities, my mum's and my granny's *manlessness* primed me to see a partner or husband as something that was not and wouldn't necessarily be attainable for me, while teenage and adolescent narratives critically held romantic heterosexual relationships in high esteem. Therefore, I understand, retrospectively, my tentativeness and low standards when I finally entered a somewhat meaningful, traditional, heterosexual, romantic relationship.

I was a twenty-year-old undergraduate student in the first term of my final year of a Politics degree when I got with Jamal. I was a virgin with ambitions to be a success in my career, but more importantly, in love. I had long established the love I had for Black men in my psyche in my early teens. I relentlessly read black urban novels that depicted love stories where societies most undesirable and shame-filled people found acceptance in the institution of love and sometimes even marriage. Unknowingly, I aligned myself with the women of these stories who were fatherless, experienced abuse, poverty, and mental health issues. I found hope in their fictitious stories of love and acceptance from men, specifically Black men.

Another element, which I identified with in their nuanced stories, were the specific types of Black men who eventually came to "save" them. Most were Black men engaged in crime and holding a subjugated place within mainstream society, while conversely, stereotypically hypermasculine and enjoying highly regarded statuses within the working-class underbelly in which they existed.[3]

All characters essentially existed on the fringes of society, and in my mind, this was how they fit together so seamlessly. As I've matured, I have learned that romantic love is indeed about acceptance, perhaps finding yourself wanting more and seeing more in your mate than they may want for or see in themselves, and romantic love is also action, which may manifest itself as care with a proclivity to protect that may look almost parental. I have also learned that we are all, including myself, innately worthy and qualify for love. However, in my then lesser informed perception of love, it looked like one person in whom I could hide, who could rid me of shame, and who could engulf me in love intense enough to renew me. And I'd happen upon this via sheer luck. The male characters in the urban romance books accepted and protected shamed and undesirable Black female characters, which made these manifestations of love poignant for me and set in my psyche that the man who would love and accept me looked equally like a Black man who existed on the fringes of society in the context within which I existed in my own marginalization.

So, at twenty years old, Jamal had been my friend (I use the term very loosely retrospectively) for a few years. I thought we were very much friends—we talked on a weekly basis and shared some painful intimate experiences with each other. Jamal introduced me to his mum and his dying grandfather while we were friends, which to me was very much an assertion of intent—I was important enough to meet these people, and so Jamal intended that I was going to be his girlfriend. A few weeks after meeting his mum, who came across as a stern, hardened, and very conservative Christian Jamaican woman, Jamal went to prison for possession of a knife. I remember feeling confused—his mum was so stern and matriarchal. I still remember the dress and matching hat she wore when I first met her, and the dominance she had over the atmosphere when she entered the house. So, how had her son fallen victim to this reality? I do not recall consciously waiting for Jamal, but I had always been in waiting for somebody to accept me. Through the Catholicism with which I was raised, the ideas my beloved late Granny had nurtured in me, and consciously seeking the church and religion when I was in university, I had developed quite conservative ideals that paralleled the belief that only a certain type of Black man would love and accept me.

Therefore, in my naive mind, a wild juxtaposition existed. I sought love and commitment, and marriage, which aligned with the safe and secure Catholicism and conservatism I respected and aspired to fit in with. But I also sought the men of the novels—that male character I conjured up in my own creative writing as a teen. I was convinced I needed a man asserting his position of power in Britain's Black working-class underbelly, because beyond it all, I just sought acceptance and to live without the self-loathing I felt.

JAMAL

Jamal for the most part, grew up in inner-city London and was exposed to a significant degree of trauma from an early age. He experienced great confusion about who his father was, and witnessed his mum move between toxic and abusive relationships. His mum's final partner and father to her last three children would disable her for the rest of her life. She married a man, Jamal remembers, who beat her in front of him and intimidated her young children with his cronies who came to play dominoes, drink, and smoke weed with their guns out on the kitchen table regularly. Being the eldest boy, they poked fun at Jamal, callously smacking him in his head for their entertainment. For Jamal, his home failed to be a place of comfort and stability. Instead, it became a place that he had to learn to navigate strategically to survive.

I will share the two most traumatic things Jamal revealed to me that highlighted different poignant types of trauma. At around eight years old, one of the cronies was using the toilet in his home. Jamal was suffering from diarrhea that day and knocked on the bathroom door in his urgency to use the toilet. He was cussed through the door and told to wait. In his nervousness and desperation, he shat himself outside of the bathroom door. The prick in the toilet emerged and laughed at him, then proceeded to descend the stairs and share his amusement at the state he found Jamal in with everybody else in the house. So, Jamal stood there, in his own shit, with roars of laughter reverberating from downstairs at his shame.

The second most poignant incident was his cousin's death. I feel stupid as I write this because I retrospectively wish I had understood this would inevitably make even the strongest and most well man, exceptionally unwell . . . it would change anybody. Jamal and his cousin were like best friends, they shared so many things in common and people even said they looked alike. Jamal was in an altercation with a young man (let's call him Q) who's bike he had bullishly taken, and Q wanted it back. Q felt violated by Jamal and the hypermasculine echo-chamber they existed in dictated that some form of intimidation ought to be used, not only for him to get his bike back but also to assert his authority over his bike and anything else he owned. Jamal and Q had a minor confrontation earlier in the day following which, Jamal decided he did not like Q's attitude. Jamal also heard through the grapevine that Q intended to demand his bike back again later that day but armed with a knife this time. Offended, Jamal intended to embarrass Q for thinking he could bully him into getting back his bike. In the early evening, Q met Jamal's cousin who decided to call Jamal hoping to mediate between the two adversaries regarding the bike. Jamal caught wind of the fact that his cousin was with Q while on the phone, and convinced his cousin to tell him where they were so he could come and give back the bike. With no intention to give the bike back, Jamal met them armed with a long plank of wood and confronted Q about the knife gossip. Jamal hit Q in the head several times with the wood, skillfully getting around his cousin with the long stick, who played piggy in the middle in an attempt to neutralize the situation and advocate for Q. Q responded by drawing for his knife, taking a wild swipe, and catching Jamal's cousin in the neck. Jamal's cousin died there, on the street.

These experiences critically shaped Jamal and the man he would become in our relationship as well as outside of it. He was violent and dangerous; finding an unhealthy high and satisfaction in engaging in violence. Much of the impenetrable loyalty and insatiable brotherly love he harped on among his friends was rooted in their common willingness to be violent as a collective. They were ever ready to sacrifice life and freedom, merely at a friend's whim. His acquaintances and friends were people who utilized this willingness to be violent under the guise of friendship and brotherhood, which, reflectively, I think Jamal believed made him a good friend. One of the first times that Jamal was open and honest with me, in the thralls of the breakdown of our relationship, he confided in me that he had shot someone with whom a friend's friend had an issue. He said he hid in the shrubbery outside of the person's home and shot them on their doorstep when they finally emerged. The last that was heard, the victim was paralyzed.

Violence, like drugs, can be used as a commodity that people trade to achieve the same goal as the drug dealer, fraudster, or robber. A study published by Birmingham City University (2015), explains that the ability to intentionally commit serious acts of violence suggest that the hitmen trading their willingness to engage in violence on this nefarious market have a dangerous and perhaps unnatural ability to dehumanize their "targets" and bury basic empathy. However, what worried me is that Jamal and the people with whom he surrounded himself, engaged in violence to satiate boredom, to ensure people still feared them, or as a release. In Jamal's life, there was often no real purpose in committing extreme acts of weaponized violence.

Jamal gained a significant reputation on the street and in prisons, also evidenced in his long criminal record. Most of the crimes he was charged with pertained to violence and possession of weapons, but more worrying was what Jamal's dysfunctional life looked like on a day-to-day basis. At the onset of our relationship, Jamal had never had a job, having not finished college and leaving school with two General Certificate of Secondary Education (GCSEs) (the national average being five). I helped him get a job and then assisted him with job applications, CVs, and cover letters religiously. Gratifyingly, Jamal went on to gain a qualification in domestic appliance maintenance during our time together. When Jamal entered the world of work, he was never able to hold onto a job for longer than a few months. Watching him navigate work life day to day, I noticed it was almost impossible for him to organize himself. While we were together, every job loss for Jamal was due to his lack of sleep, poor maintenance of work equipment, and overall poor workmanship. Jamal was insistent on juggling *the roads* and a normal life. The roads brought with them their own toxicity and dysfunction that ruled Jamal's existence.

Now, I see how vulnerable Jamal actually was and how the violence masked and protected the deep vulnerability he felt. As a child, Jamal felt powerless. He both experienced and witnessed acts of intimidation and violence used to punish and assert power. Ill-equipped adult Jamal navigated relationships that necessitated trust and vulnerability with destructive tendencies that kept his learned behaviors intact.

An additional element in Jamal's life, undeniably problematic to love and romantic relationships, was the cesspit of misogyny he blindly celebrated. Extremes are depicted in the music industry, for example, R. Kelly's cult, but on a microlevel, these men, Jamal included, exist in an echo chamber where they subscribe to the view that women ought not to be trusted. He believed the female body existed as a commodity for men's pleasure. Unfortunately, my past relationship with Jamal proves that Black men like this are a problematic patriarch actively exerting power over Black working-class women. This was highlighted during a conversation with Jamal where he felt it was crucial to let me know that his friend intended to "start a brothel." In my nuanced disgust and intrigue at his audacity, I probed, asking where and how would he find women to work in his brothel? To which Jamal flippantly suggested particular types of women could be encouraged to comply. I challenged this. He became frustrated. Conversation over.

I AM JADE

As I mentioned, I grew up feeling like having a man was something I wouldn't be able to accomplish easily, stemming from realities I saw around me. I come from a matriarchal family with my granny and then my mum at the helm as protector and provider. This was reinforced by most of my mum's sisters who were unmarried single mothers (bar one). My mum was a single mother from my birth, but my father's absence was far more complex than a simple lack of presence for a plethora of reasons. My father was absent but still visible. I would see him somewhat regularly as he had a friend who lived four doors from my childhood home. At this time, we lived on a hill with our front windows facing the mouth of the hill. I would watch for hours what was going on in the street and see my father driving up the hill, blaring music, and parking obnoxiously in the middle of the road. He would then visit his friend, hop back in his car, and drive off. I watched him do this for many of my formative years from my windowsill. Other memories that cal-cified the inevitable void fatherlessness brought with it were the times I begged my mum to call him, which she obliged. On occasion, he agreed to come around and pick me up. Many times, he never showed up. On these occasions I would then beg my mum to let me call him to see where he was or remind him of our plans (calls that were ignored), and even plead with her to walk me to the bottom of the hill to look out for him. My mum gratified my innocent desperation, giving in to my requests, but these experiences eroded my self-worth and lowered my expectations. My father also had another family during my childhood, so as a child suffering his absenteeism, a deafening confusion tainted my view of family. I wondered why he was a father to my half-sister and brother but wasn't a father to me.

I also remember the role he played in the first time I felt like I was a disgusting being.[4] On one of the few fraught occasions when he visited, requiring mum to endure his presence like a saint, my father turned to my mum and asked her why my belly was so big, then turned to me and asked me if my stomach was filled with poo. I was no older than seven at the time, but I remember feeling visceral discomfort and embarrassment at my little free and innocent seven-year-old body. That discomfort and feeling that I was undesirable became a part of me. When I eventually had some form of agency and acquired the capacity to decide the direction my life would go, I actively sought ways to add value to myself and essentially make myself worthier and more desirable. Key ways I tried to validate myself were work-ing several jobs, engaging in career-focused opportunities, going to the gym, actively trying to grow my hair, and buying lots of on trend clothing. Uncon-sciously, I was convinced that if I became a slimmer Jade with longer natural hair, clear skin, and loads of clothes, an impressive CV, my own money, and a university degree, *then*, and only then, would I be worthy of and qualify for love.

Choosing Jamal was admittedly somewhat manipulative, and I thought I was making a fool-proof choice. I was moderately aware of his past challenges and aside from a somewhat narcissistic belief that I would be able to help him, I also strongly believed that he would surely appreciate me, as I had added value unto myself so much more than he had added unto himself. I also felt that journeying with Jamal and helping him add value to himself would add a new dimension to my value as a woman in his eyes. I expected Jamal would look at what I had helped him achieve, inevitably making him love and appreciate me more. At that point in my life, love existed as something I had to work to earn outwardly rather than something I was worthy of innately. My inadequacies however, didn't exist in a vacuum. Maybe, I might have viewed myself in a better light or perhaps chosen better paths if not for other external realities further pushing me down the paths I walked.

SELF-ESTEEM IN LOVE

Self-esteem is what one believes they can accomplish, how they view themselves, and what they believe they deserve. In the context of a romantic relationship, self-esteem is central to how one navigates the pitfalls and terrain of intimacy. It will influence what one accepts, the boundaries one puts in place, the extent to which one enforces and refuses to waive their boundaries, and the point at which one decides a relationship may be failing to satisfy important desires and expectations. Someone with high self-esteem is typically more comfortable instituting boundaries in relationships and may see a partner's failure or disinterest in fulfilling what they reasonably believe they deserve as apt grounds to end a relationship. Self-esteem informs the qualities and characteristics one expects to see in their partners and emboldens us with the tenacity to hold our partners accountable when they are falling short. In the realm of romance, self-esteem may be more commonly referred to as "standards."

Self-esteem is important in my narrative for a plethora of reasons. Firstly, I see retrospectively, that my self-esteem was dangerously latent. My view of myself was exceptionally distorted. I was unsure of what I deserved and found it almost impossible to assert my expectation of the bare minimum. A healthy and respectful relationship was something I increasingly began to believe was not in my reach and in turn, Jamal was able to progressively erode my already loosely imposed boundaries and convince me that my assertions were unfounded, unfair, and unattractive. To provide better context, Jamal, from his midteens onward, was essentially part of a London gang. He gravitated between being an intimidating and respected member of the gang while simultaneously playing the role of a serious potential life partner committed to reforming and improving his life. On several occasions Jamal ghosted for hours, at times overnight, popping back up and refusing to fully explain where he had been. When I attempted to initiate conversations about effective communication going forward, Jamal would essentially refuse under the guise of protecting me, protecting his *mandem*, and protecting himself. Jamal's lies went as far as convincing me that due to my innocent nature, he couldn't tell me anything regarding what he was doing because the police could question me under a lie detector test and I would fail it. Of course, the Metropolitan police don't even use polygraph tests.

Where misogyny exists, the perception that women ought to accept bad behavior and deserve to be cast as a bad partner if they are not forgiving and understanding thrives. For example, a pop cultural reference is the Offset and Cardi B relationship drama that seemed to last for months. In 2018, Offset was once more exposed as a cheat, resulting in his wife Cardi B (who is in many ways considered more successful than him) ending their relationship. In response, many predominantly Black male celebrities went out of their way to publicly advocate on behalf of Offset and plead with Cardi B to take him back. She was cast as coldhearted, unsupportive, and unbending, especially after Offset made some emotional and grand gestures of repentance. Similarly, Jamal's friends and family played a key role in advocating on his behalf to convince me to stay, forgive, and endure. They implored me to extend my compassion and understanding, and to work hard to meet Jamal wherever he moved the goalpost. I can't speak for Cardi B, I can only express my opinion while reflecting on my own experiences, but both instances reflect significant displays of lacking self-esteem. Neither of us were able to uphold important boundaries and remain steadfast in our decisions around what is acceptable and permissible. Instead, we allowed ourselves to be convinced that how we view ourselves and what we deserve is unreasonable and a good woman is one who will accept a flawed man and work hard to make him better.

My acquiescence further fueled the extent and frequency with which Jamal manipulated the relationship, and me, to work as he desired. By the end of the relationship, I carried an abundance of shame and self-disdain looking at what had become normalized, how much I failed to hold Jamal accountable, and the fear I had developed for his reactions and retorts. I think back to an occasion in the last few weeks of our relationship where we traveled to visit a friend of mine, Elle, living abroad. One evening, myself, Elle, Jamal, and Elle's husband went to eat from some street vendors in the barrio. On our way back, Jamal revealed to Elle and I that he had brought one of Elle's kitchen knives out, concealed in his shorts, "just in case." I was absolutely mortified. Elle, her husband, Elle's family, and her husband's family are the least violent, most law-abiding people you'd ever meet, so what did Jamal think they would do if he stabbed someone? Assist him in disposing of the weapon? Provide him with an escape route? That evening was the first time in a while that I attempted to hold Jamal accountable to his actions. I quietly spoke to him with no one else around and explained that they were not knife-carrying, criminal types; and in most likelihood they would have both had heart attacks on the spot if he had brandished the knife at a bandit. I also pointed out we both lacked knowledge of gangs, policing, and even the geography of the country, let alone the barrio we had been in, at that point, for barely a week. Jamal was incredibly offended and acted affronted. He looked and spoke to me like I was dumb, told me I was wrong, and insisted he had unequivocally done the most right and logical thing in bringing the knife. I just dropped the topic.

One of the saddest elements of my relationship with Jamal was my genuine belief that Jamal was my best friend, despite the way he treated me and the things he did, which was a further manifestation of my low self-esteem. At the time, I was unable to see that Jamal preferred a situation that lacked boundaries where I didn't tell him "no!" It was in his interest to convince me that he was my best friend and knew me better than I knew myself because it ensured I remained subservient to his desire to do whatever he wanted, inconsequentially. The consequences were mine as I lived with a lack of sureness in myself, in what I was seeing, and what I knew to be true. The situation worsened for me over time as I continued to believe he was my friend even if he disrespected my boundaries, weakened my resolve, and my self-esteem continued to erode.

The insidious erasure of who I was is frightening as I reflect. It began intentionally so that he could engage freely in criminal and violent gang life. Jamal manipulated a relationship where I could never criticize, comment, or pose ultimatums, and although much of his criminality was hidden, when cracks began to show, Jamal used emotional manipulation and threats to stop me from expressing my opinions or desires. Looking back, this commenced early on, during a stretch in prison in the first year of our relationship. Jamal was carted off to prison out of the blue one September night. I did not find out the allegations against him until several weeks later via his very unprofessional solicitor, but Jamal was on remand, accused of fighting and then stabbing a man in broad daylight in front of innocent members of the public. The actual details of the crime were never admitted or revealed to me by him until many years later. I had always said I wouldn't stick around if Jamal went to prison, but I did, activating the erosion of boundaries and respect as I failed to keep my word and hold him accountable.

There was also the case of Jamal's car, which he allowed his friend, Terry, to unofficially "rent" from him during his stretch in prison. It was arranged that Terry would meet me weekly and give me £50 while he used the car. Within two weeks of the commencement of this agreement a letter arrived at Jamal's mum's house—the car had been impounded. Terry initially denied the car had been impounded insisting that the letter was mistakenly sent and that the car was parked outside of his home. After about two weeks, Terry finally admitted that the car had been towed while illegally parked. By this time the impound fee was over £500. Naturally, I offered to pay the fee and just needed Terry to accompany me to the pound as he was the only driver insured on the vehicle. Terry disappeared. Jamal lost his car. When I attempted to speak to Jamal about his friendship with Terry and the lack of care, concern, and compassion Terry displayed in the situation, Jamal viciously warned me to never speak ill of his friends. He told me I should never attempt to "get in between" him and his friends and I should never attempt to compare the things I was willing to do for him with what I witnessed his friends doing. From then on, during arguments or conflicts, Jamal refused to respect my boundaries because, he claimed, I attempted to criticize his friend Terry. Given his loyalty to a friend who lost him his car, lied, and disappeared, Jamal was far from a friend to me. In fact, Jamal's behavior was arguably that of someone who despised me. What is most poignant retrospectively is the immense lack of love I had for myself and the poverty in my judgment around what a friend and partner ought to be.

CONCLUSION

I do not suppose that men like Jamal don't deserve love. I don't even believe that men like Jamal don't deserve love from progressive, aspirational, and professional Black women. We all innately deserve love and in light of their trauma's, I hope men like Jamal receive love in large measure. I think this foundational awareness and belief possibly fueled me in my actions when I loved Jamal the most—when he needed to be understood, listened to, and nurtured in the simplest ways. However, I don't think Black women should tolerate abuse, misogynoir, or operate from a place of fear and lack. There is power in our refusal to accept and settle which will stand to pull Black men up by their bootstraps.

I started this piece essentially working through why I chose Jamal from a personal standpoint, but my reflections are informed by social, economic, and political externalities. This was an important task and an opportunity for me to delve into my younger self from a more informed perspective and explore my decisions. I embarked on this initially from a place of frustration because I am terrible at forgiving myself and granting myself grace, and so this piece served as an important way to soothe my frustrations with a reasoned discussion exploring why I chose Jamal.

By the time I made the decision to finally end the relationship, friendship, and any other form of interaction with Jamal, he had cheated, bullied, and gaslighted me into someone uncertain, untrusting of my own judgment, and fearful of posing challenges. I was so fearful and anxious having been fed, for years, wild narratives and manipulative lies about rival gangs and police-centered conspiracies to harm and catch him, and sometimes, me too. Jamal cruelly boasted about his violent and madcap capabilities making me fear what he may do to me but also to others and himself if I did not "behave accordingly." I became responsible for his behavior and criminality. Without delving further into the abyss I fortunately escaped. This essay has been redemptive in that it stands to provide an avenue for understanding, not just to myself but to the people I indirectly hurt while enduring the "love" I sought. I hope this essay will assist on the journey back to self that young Black BEAUTIFUL women may embark on *before* seeking to love and be loved by equally beautiful Black men.

Please love yourself foremost.

NOTES

1. "Yardie" refers to a Jamaican, but in working-class British culture, describing someone or people as "yardie" would suggest they possess a particular temperament, style of dress, boldness among other attitudinal and stylistic attributes.

2. My mum had two very short-lived but abusive encounters with men who resided abroad for large parts of the year.

3. I utilize the phrase "working-class underbelly" throughout this piece as it denotes a group, comprising mostly ethnic minorities residing in the UK. Statistically they would be described as working class, however, their existence is significantly different to what would traditionally be described as working class due to the higher instances of exclusion/school dropout/criminality/lower incomes/higher sociopolitical engagement and so on.

4. By disgusting I mean an extreme sense of undesirability pertaining specifically to how I looked physically. My perception of my body specifically became pertinent and influenced my self-perception and how I would assume I was perceived by others.

REFERENCES

Banks, R. R. (2011). *Is Marriage for White People? How the African American Marriage Decline Affects Everyone.* United Kingdom: Plume.

Barker, P. (1996, April). How many black men have white partners? *The Independent.*

Birmingham City University. (2015). *The Psychology of Assassins: Hitmen Bury Their Feelings for a Successful Kill.* https://www.ethnicity-facts-figures.service.gov.uk/education-skills-and-training/11-to-16-years-old/percentage-achieving-a-c-in-english-and-maths/latest.

Department for Education. (2017). *A* to C in English and Maths GCSE Attainment for Children Aged 14 to 16 (Key Stage 4).* Cabinet Office: United States.

Francisco, E. (2017). *How Tinder Accidentally Exposed Society's Inherent Racism.* New York: Inverse:.

HESA. (2018). *Higher Education Student Statistics: UK, 2016/17—Student numbers and characteristics.* HESA: United Kingdom.

Hunte, B. (2017, March). London's black male graduates less likely to get jobs. United Kingdom: *BBC News.*

National Statistics. (2017). *Statistics on Race and the Criminal Justice System 2016. United Kingdom:* Ministry of Justice.

Petter, O. (2018, August). Racism is rife on dating apps—where does it come from and how can it be fixed? United States: *The Independent*.

Song, M. (2009). Is intermarriage a good indicator of integration? *Journal of Ethnic and Migration Studies, 35*(2), 331–348. United Kingdom.

Chapter Four

Emotional Storms and Black Intimacies

Michael Baugh

The shards of our intimate affiliations find their moment of fracture in the trauma-laden anti-Black implantations littering our psychic landscape.

In this illumination, the debris of our affinities are but the fruits of most deleterious and utilitarian performances manifesting on the social stage.

Performances these are which, when brought to spaces most intimate, desiccate the vitality of our bonds.

Unfolding routines and conflicts are fed by our failure to completely re-press and digest the trauma rooted in an anti-Black society.

Collectively, this catalyzes certain "annihilative forces," indiscreetly pruning and castrating areas of our psychic space; and in a crawling instant we find our most intimate relations captured by a destructive dénouement,

Which we come to realize has already brought our coupling to the door of a wounding conclusion.

And in time, some may come to realize that their "ways of being" in the world,

Alongside their reactionary mechanisms to the world, ceaselessly alters their "ways of being" with one another.

(Baugh, unpublished)

I never met my mother;
Only did I encounter the strength she placed in between us.
I never met my father;
Only did I encounter the distancing silence he placed in between us.
And as I grew into adulthood,
I become more confident that they never met one another.
They are forever strangers who remain legally bound for the "appearance" of unity,
A reality that is often misinterpreted as Black love.
(Baugh, unpublished)

WORKING THROUGH EMOTIONAL STORMS

Michael Eigen (2005) reminds us that it was W. R. Bion (1994/1979) who once divulged, "When two personalities meet, an emotional storm is created" (p. 321). And this "Emotional storm," Michael Eigen, would write, "is something basic—like grief, anger, fear, joy, any of which can be stormlike" (p. 19). Yet it is necessary that we understand, the advent of the "Emotional storm, is not pathology. It is part of reactivity, permeability, responsiveness—part of what happens when people meet. . . . We create storms in each other" (Eigen, 2005, pp. 19–20). For the storm, in essence, is that "mysterious something," which erupts as a result of our encounter with other beings. From cradle to grave our encounters with other beings cannot help but endlessly alter our atmospheric pressure, our psychic humidity.

Beings change us, erect within us storms, which bring warm humid psychic air to our, at times, cool zones; and soon degrees of precipitation follow along with thunderous roars. Perturbed we are by the tempest, which erects once sunken ships to the surface of our consciousness. Mercilessly, the cyclone will not allow bodies, anthropologically rooted, or not, to rest in the grave. Our encounter with one another will do that. It will not allow the buried to remain hidden. Storms have a way of disturbing the psychic seabed. In such a mystifying way, the storm forces us to feel that which we dare not to, that which we have quarantined. Dead or dormant zones come alive once more and we are again cast out to sea. The psychic current pulls us back into the region of tumult, the instability of the wave. And there is terrifying anxiety in this.

REFLECTIONS ON EIGEN

A terrifying chaos erupts during and after the storm because our powers of "selective permeability" exist . . . not.

We must contend with that which initiates forces which, we feel, disassemble us because these forces render apart our feeling of wholeness.

We must recognize the full breadth of the psychic and somatic, or at least what little we can.

We must feel each chord on the scale of feeling as it releases a mystifying experience we have not the means or maturity to confidently grasp.

But, what are we to do when our cup or well of emotion runneth over?

Here, our inexperience and inability become more evident.

Here, we are proved rather powerless.

Here, unaddressed storms linger, raging on, seeming to wage war on our inner landscapes.

Here, the eye of Jupiter continues its onslaught, engulfing minor squalls, floating with intention, swallowing up aspects of self in places we know not where.

Here, our encounters with others bring forth a sort of cosmic chaos.

Here, the cosmos within us play on, seemingly with the spontaneous narratives of our lives dictating and impacting each event.

Then, cosmos within us are endlessly ripe with collisions and furious activity.

Then, a greater "emotional maturity" (Eigen, 2005; Eigen & Goyrin, 2007) awaits if we seek not to prune the vines of feeling.

But what does it mean to travel down what appears to be a rabbit hole of feeling? What will this do to us? We must meditate on what it means "to stay open to the impact of the other, whatever gets set off" (Eigen, 2005, pp. 58–59).

Our romantic partners set off something within.
Follow it.
A rollercoaster awaits.
Follow it.
Where will it lead?
Follow it.
I know not where.
Follow it.
We will be altered.
Follow it.

The sea of emotion is the unpredictable Poseidon that is life. Yes, what does it look like to "follow the impact through its transformations" (Eigen, 2005, p. 59)? The thought alone startles. For will that which we shall find overwhelm us: a tsunami of emotion? Eigen (2005) has outlined the consequences of thwarting our negating psychic emotion and its impact on our ability to digest current and future storms. And we know—"Impact (shock waves) gives rise to feelings, to images, to thoughts, to . . . an ever-undulating series of states involving unconscious transmissions, imaginative visions" (Eigen, 2005, p. 59). This is seemingly unfiltered chaos. Disorder. Yet always does the infinite power of emotional roots, vines, break through the makeshift concrete of the sanitized and orderly existence we attempt to construct.

Jesus was touched on the hem of his garment. "Who touched me?"[1] He responded to the touch of another. To this we must attend.

Eigen (2005) illuminates our discomfort in the face of an ever-churning beautiful concoction of unnerving feelings, which leave us gyrating between wholeness and desolidification. Eigen (2005) is stressing a sensitivity to the rhizomatic corridors crossed, sojourned, and excited by our infinite collisions with one another, other beings. And from this we run away. From such we attempt, mightily, to avoid the unnerving emotions, which arise from our psychic nerve endings. Simply, "we try to regulate the more, the flood of events, the emotional flood" (Eigen & Goyrin, 2007, p. 45).

But, I must reiterate, we *shan't* run from the storm.

Bion, cited by Eigen (2005), pushes for us to have a sort of "patience" with ourselves. What does this entail but to bathe in the waters of *feeling* what feeling does to us? This entails a commitment to the rollercoaster, a commitment to hearing and feeling as much of (what I term) the psychic scale in all its musicality as possible so that, as according to Eigen (2005), we may become more emotionally mature.

Yet, what is absent in Eigen's (2005) ruminations is how such storm-invoking experiences join with the profoundly racial and gendered realities befalling the dispersed descendants of the African continent. In other words, what is missing is a delving into the uniqueness of the storm as it relates to Black beings. Eigen (2005) suggests that we "follow the impact through its transformations" (p. 59). And to this I agree most assuredly. But I wonder, for Black bodies, such as myself, if we were to follow the impact(s), where would they lead, except, ultimately, to a place most traumatic? Where would they lead, except, ultimately, to the terror of colonization, and bring to the fore the reality that we are still living in a storm of a different kind? In this, I wish to evoke the collective memory of Black folk as I make plain.

Hurricane Katrina did not make landfall in 2005. It has been present since African's became slaves. For Black bodies have long had to wade in the waters of social abandonment. Yet overall, I believe Black psychic life to always, in some way, be a laborious traumatic return to the haunting "door of no return" of which Dionne Brand (2002) speaks. Every interaction with the world, in some fashion, reminds us that we remain shackled in the *hold of the ship* (Wilderson, 2010). It reminds us of our existence, still, *in the wake* of the ship (Sharpe, 2016).

Storms often transport Black people back to a traumatic place. Injustices and inequities seem to always further agitate our wounds of exclusion. The Black man's collision with the Black woman reminds, for example, of our existence in the hold of the ship. We don't talk about it. We blind ourselves to the actuality of our reality. It hurts. And in this, we abruptly close the door to feeling. In the end, we close the door upon one another.

Our manner of coping results in us damming up our emotional springs (more accurately, I refer to the blocking of sentiments, which would reveal any degree of vulnerability/anything that can be read as weakness). And, in the end the consequence is that we shut the door to greater exploration of self and partner. And we wonder what is wrong. In this, I ask that we engage in doing the difficult work of identifying and articulating that pain. I mean not to travel too far ahead of myself, but I wish to make clear that Black bodies, for good reason, find ways to avoid and marginalize the emotional storms that arise. We seek shelter from the storm too often. And this be the crux: the methods of avoidance, often employed by many a Black being, are unique to Black bodies. For one may avoid the storm under the assumption that this is how they will endure, or "make it," to the following day. And, I posit, that these methods employed by Black people are simultaneously the very tools of their survival/that which is chiefly responsible for their persistence in an anti-Black world, and that which aides in their psychic-emotional destruction. Worth extracting here, I believe the *methods of self-protection* constructed by many a Black body to be destructive to the longevity of their most intimate relations.

I understand that the point from which I launch is indeed a theoretical lens rooted in White psychological discourse. Yet such a lens cannot, as is, be used without alteration or rearticulation when concerning Black bodies. Therefore, I seek to communicate the intentions behind Eigen's (1996) work while seasoning such with African American spices to construct a narrative in which Europe is not, again, overtly judging and disciplining African-rooted bodies. I choose to make Black heterosexual relations and relationship dissolution or spousal dissimilarity, which I describe as relational ruptures in the lives of Black folk, my focus. To do this effectively, I believe it is necessary to look at the Black person's response to emotional storms. Storms arise from our collisions with the "White and Brown" world. Storms arise in the interaction between Black partners. We, Black people, erect defensive selves to manage, quarantine, or destroy these storms. Understandably, we place upon our person a mask—which we also wear at bedtime, to protect ourselves from the world that antagonizes us, to protect ourselves from our inner storms, to hide from one another.

A sign reads: Do Not Disturb.

We seek to abbreviate or lessen the sensitivity of our psychic nerve endings. Unfortunately, these acts have a lasting impact on how we as Black people interact with each other, the very decisions we make in choosing a partner. Perhaps we as Black people can ponder on how we can alter, somewhat, the nature of our impacts on each other as we experience various onslaughts from the dangerous sociopolitical realm.

AND NOW FOR MY STORY

I am putting forth that there is something to unearth in the performance of the "strong Black woman" (SBW), and there is something to interrogate within what Majors and Billson (1992) moniker the "cool pose," which speaks of a performance displayed by many a Black male. I am choosing to label this the cool-Black-male (CBM) framework, that will allow me to better articulate the topography of black dissimilarity/uncoupling. Examining these two performances will help me to explain Black uncoupling as I have witnessed it. And throughout, I will refer to these as destructive performances; for they have a part to play in the survival of Black people but are ultimately destructive to their mental and psychic health and present a damaging impact on romantic partnering.

Through reflections on my parents' coupling, I seek to illuminate the atmospheric conditions that may contribute to the collapse of Black intimate relations. And as I discuss the SBW and CBM, I keep in mind that I am not pathologizing Black people, neither am I blaming them for what is evident in so many of their lives. I place the blame at the feet of whiteness and consider what the racial world has erected within all people; how a lack of criticality increases the possibility for all us to engage in acts of symbolic and psychic violence upon ourselves and upon one another. As I address the emotional life of the SBW and CBM, I am not concluding that there was absolutely no sign of emotional life in my parents. Instead, I am arguing that a conundrum exists to a degree in the psychic life, which is traumatic for Black couples. Feeling is understandably abbreviated. Yet, healthy romantic relations will not rise out of such abbreviations. Healthy relationships cannot thrive in the shadow of heroic performances of strength and coolness.

MY MOTHER, DIANA

"My name is De'Aja, and I am a ssttrroonngg Black woman," one of my students proclaimed on the first day of class, and I asked her what she meant (since I am always interested in hearing the explanations). "It means, I'm strong," she said. I saw that she had not understood my probing for depth and so I responded, "Give me more. What does this entail?" She responded, "I'm independent and strong-minded, and I don't put up with no sh*t." She's an eighteen-year-old freshman. That's young. I am reminded somehow of my mother, now in her sixties, who has long embodied much of the framework presented by De'Aja. Like De'Aja, the composition of my mother's "strength" was to show a defiant face to the world, an intimidating power, an unmatched resilience. She desired a superhuman aura while carrying a moral compass. My mother, Diana, painted herself as an Atlas figure, the Christ-like bearer of burden, burdens both real and imagined, while never breaking her SBW character.

Even more than De'Aja, my mother wished to evoke an endless display of fantastic feats on the trip wire while juggling inequity and hardship on a unicycle. I still say, to this day, it is the greatest show on Earth, or more accurately—in the Western world. A show with dual effect. It tantalizes the viewer, while further hypnotizing the performer to clasp tighter their grip on the framework of strength. Yet what great magicians these SBW are, that arise in the Black community. They are heralded for "making something out of nothing"—something I've heard my mother's associates and girlfriends proclaim. Often, I wonder what took more courage and strength—directly dealing with deteriorating intimate relations with my father, confronting conflicts within oneself, or committing to the superhuman identity. Of course, each time I tried to push my mother into examining what was taking place within her—I was always very sensitive to these things—she cursed me and shewed me away. I have long wondered what was on the other side of her psychic moon. My mother often told me, explicitly, "I do the best I can. I put a roof over your damn head. And I'm not putting up with crap from you. I have a scar on my stomach. See it? I gave birth to you. I have this scar because of you. I work all day. I gave you this. I bought you that. I put you in good schools. And I gotta take care of everything for everybody. Nobody's gonna do it. Your stupid father sure won't help." She cast herself as the essential caregiver for all immediate and extended family members; overextending herself greatly as she hurried to the homes of all who she believed needed her. Too, she was the Christlike bearer of the emotional weight of the world—never letting you forget that she was like Christ. And like Christ, she was "wounded," though it be cesarean, it was a pain she endured for others.

It is the "StrongBlackWoman," as Walker-Barnes (2017) phrases it (intentional truncation by Walker-Barnes), that is "a very specific way of being in the world" (in Evans, Bell, and Burton, 2017, p. 44). This very specific way of "being in the world" appears born out of historical violence and trauma (Abrams et al., 2018; Nelson et al., 2016; Shorter-Gooden et al., 1996). Appearing most evident, "the strong black woman is an affirming symbol" and puts on display a superhuman ability and willingness to face the challenges impressed upon her by what is essentially the crosshairs of her intersectional position (Harris-Lacewell, 2001, p. 4). In echo of Harris-Lacewell (2001), Abrams et al. (2018) posit the emergence and perpetuation of the SBW as stemming from the realities and experiences brought about by intersectional oppression, which most assuredly stem from the years of formal bondage. Yet, what is evident in this is that the SBW is "a racialized gender performance, a scripted role into which Black women are socialized" (Walker- Barnes, 2014, p. 4).

Always with this "strength" Diana revealed moments of intense rage—a breakdown accompanied by violence. Oh yes, there was great violence. Much of the literature articulates that the SBW will be reluctant to showcase her anger, in fear it will demonstrate a lack of control and composure. Yet, Regina Romero (2000) reveals that intense anger can be shown if the SBW considers the recipient of that anger—a "safe target"—certain male partners and children whom she perceives as behaving in ways she deems unacceptable (p. 229). My mother presented aspects of the stereotypical strong Black woman which was further complicated by her borderline personality tendencies. I lean toward suggesting that borderline tendencies are not distant from the framework but more so integrated within the framework because in the shadow of emotional composure microbursts of rage can erupt.

From an early age, many Black women are encouraged to "draw attention away from hurt and refocus . . . on tasks and responsibilities at hand" (Beauboeuf-Lafontant, 2009, p. 78). In the background echoes: "If feeling life is sat on, it does not have the chance to evolve" (Eigen, 2005, p. 21). Often, emotional life is sat on and our romantic efforts fail to evolve. But do SBW sit upon their emotional life and tend to the needs of others because in each instance the needs of others appear more immediate, or do these women often sit on feeling life and tend to others because they do not know what to do with the tumultuous waves within them? During much of the day Diana oscillated between a cantankerous cocktail of ire littered with traces of despair and that stoic hero of legend, the more conventional SBW, who was willing to take on the world to defend and uplift those closest to her. I admit, she performed mighty feats. She placed enormous tasks and immense responsibilities in her own hands and labored to persevere on that road to the cross. Certainly "managing multiple roles was seen as a marker of one's strength and fortitude." Walker-Barnes (2014) adds as she concludes, "Industriousness and busy-ness were highly esteemed characteristics among Black Baptist women" (p. 105). My mother aspired to be a strong Christian-Baptist woman. With this, I must include, "a 'real' Black woman" is described as "a StrongBlackWoman—autonomous, industrious, reliable, and capable" (Walker-Barnes, 2014, p. 106). She remains always at the disposal of the Black community and at the disposal of those in the White workplace (Beauboeuf-Lafontant, 2009).

Mother performed her part well. But there is something within my mother's performance that I wish to highlight for the purposes of our text. In a moment of transparency, I admit: I have never really met my mother. I've never had the opportunity to get to know her. I only ever encountered the "strength" she placed in between us. She wore many hats. She endured socioeconomic struggle. She was all things to all people. And I saw evidence of her SBW persona cracking; but I never encountered the very being that lies beneath the surface. She never let me in. And what of my father? He has hurt her, before my birth, in some way. I don't know the specifics. He lies often. He plays it cool. She decides to hurt him. Violence arises. Is it always him that incites her rage? Was it the demand to remain faithful to the tenets of the SBW? Was it what he placed upon her? Was it what she placed upon herself?

Romero (2000) divulges that the SBW unconsciously avoids intimate relations with "kind, gentle men who are emotionally mature," citing the fear of intimacy and more importantly what that intimacy with emotionally mature men will do: that is—expose the "vulnerabilities such as fear, self-doubt, shame, and hurt" (Romero, 2000, p. 230). These SBW, according to Romero, tend to be drawn to men whose "personal or professional growth has somehow been curtailed" (Romero, 2000, p. 239). Then they proceed to embark upon the task of repairing the broken and incompetent male. Notice in this, though the SBW may not be in the relationship she envisioned, the SBW can assume her role as fixer, leader, savior. She can keep her vulnerability and safety intact. In all honesty, this is the relationship of my mother and father. My mother sought, at all costs, to avoid the emotional waves and rising tides of her inner world in her relationship. I saw her at work over the years. She was always guarded. I understood the impact of the White world as I grew older. I watched her at home. She remained guarded. Could she not see that this was hurting her in *this* arena, under this roof? "It was much easier for her to assert her wishes for the household than it was to express her wishes for their relationship," Romero reflects (Romero, 2000, p. 230). The latter sort of communication put my mother at risk for exposure.

I realize that my relationship with her existed as a parent-child relation but I can remember no instance, even into adulthood, in which she was open and honest, genuine, and forthcoming with me. To be vulnerable was, to her, a crime. Each time I tried to discuss anything beyond the superficial, I was met with opposition. All she ever spoke to my father about was the superficial. The facade of a relationship, this lie of togetherness, still disturbs me. Each instance in which I exposed a crack in her armor, she cursed me and ran away. I asked too many questions. I probed too much. I "did not know my place" she would respond. She rushed to save face, to immediately place some sort of psychic plaster on her cracking emotional walls. She quelled what I assume had erupted within her. I saw signs of cracking, but she never discussed it. She never allowed the make-up of "strength" to come off. Beauboeuf-Lafontant (2009) describes this strength as "a demand" and "self-protective strategy" that requires "Black women act as if they were invulnerable to abuse" (p. 7). The SBW schema on display is not an authentic display of the depths of their emotional persona. Instead "it is a mask that stifles authenticity, subsuming multifaceted selves behind a singular wall of self-sacrifice and emotional stoicism" (Walker-Barnes, 2014, p. 4). We never shared a genuine experience.

I say all of this to make plain: I think about the men who probe too much, who ask too many questions, who seek a genuine experience. I wonder how many Black boys have never had the opportunity to meet their mothers. More appropriate in this context, I wonder how many Black men are privileged enough to meet the women with whom they are dating or share a marriage. I doubt my father, who was and is just as troubling, ever met my mother. I doubt he wished to meet her (a meeting would incite a storm). I never witnessed her letting him in or vice versa. I only witnessed the moral pedestal on which she stood and looked down upon him. I only witnessed his absence in her presence. And I wonder what happens to a relationship, when one fails to meet the person with whom they have exchanged vows. Strength, for my mother, created a chasm, which allowed no one to visit her psychological locale and share in her emotional experience. Strength, for her, was to deny and redirect vulnerability and breakdown. Strength, for her, was in maintaining the material world for her children, while forsaking the quality of the interpersonal connections.

And still I wonder about De'Aja. Will De'Aja become like my mother? Will De'Aja submerge her emotional life? Will she do this violence to herself? Will she allow a young man to enter her life but only on the outskirts of her world? Will she allow her future mate the opportunity to meet her in genuine and intimate ways? What do the De'Aja's of the world do to men who probe too much, who ask too many questions? Will she emote, genuinely?

To be transparent, one of the things that hinders my intimate relations with women is my intellectualization of almost all conversation that I feel would lead to vulnerable places within me. My intellectualization is my "safe room," which of course by definition bars others from invasion or bars uncomfortable feelings from saturating the landscape and possibly being absorbed by the psychic roots. What if I were to absorb feelings that would disassemble me, make me feel less whole? Was I ever whole to begin with? Eigen (2005) cites that our tendency to rationalize emotions is an effort to "tone down their ability to disturb" (pp. 20–21). I wonder what the SBW does to temper her emotions, redirect her feelings and attention. Is she laboring to tone down their ability to disturb, to disrupt their facade? "She relies upon the defense mechanisms of denial, repression, and suppression to contain negative affect," Walker-Barnes reveals, "creating a mental and emotional dam behind which she blocks off negative affect" (in Evans et al., 2017, p. 44). This is but an attempt to arrest the storm. Walker-Barnes adds that any breach or crack in the dam of the SBW "might unleash the flood of emotionality behind it" (in Evans et al., 2017, p. 44). Strength's commanding image and manipulative grip can compromise the psyches of Black women (Beauboeuf-Lafontant, 2009) and places great strain on their interpersonal relations (Woods-Giscombé, 2010). Vulnerability bleeds through the stonewalling. She attempts to cover the cracks as the CBM rushes to cover his own.

CARL STRIKES A COOL POSE

"Carl, say something. SAY SOMETHING! SAY SOMETHING! Why won't you respond? Stop looking at me. Say something, dammit." Hurling aggression wildly, this was my mother's response to what I describe as my father's *catatonic cool*. Cool, is that which "appear[s] indifferent to the problems around him or seem impervious to pain, frustration, or death" (Majors and Billson, 1992, p. 28). My father's *cool*, always reinforced by his antisocial personality behaviors, and further complicated by what appeared to be epi-sodes of catatonic behavior at home, was endlessly a destabilizing force in his marriage. He was and is a walking corpse. A hollowed being. I wondered where he had gone, when he had vacated the premises. I looked for him. I never found him. He was never present at home. His body sat at the dinner table, but there was no one I could see that was occupying his fleshly vessel. I never met my father. I only came to know his emotional distance, his unwillingness to go beyond superficial conversation with just a few words, and his stifling silence. He did not speak to his children. He spoke only when angered or forced. I say this not from a child's naïveté but because these are crimes with which my mother charged him. I admit, she was and is complete-ly accurate. As a young teen, I began to imagine and moniker my father the Wizard of a very different Oz; for he did everything he could, sometimes with flits of unexpected rage "to cover his anguish" (Majors and Billson, 1992, p. 44) and to keep everyone from looking beneath the surface. During my teenage years, I learned to not follow the white-tiled path to the room he mostly resided in. He remained at a great distance from the world in which his children and wife inhabited.

My father did not have the academic or technical skills to be an economic provider. My mother, at least, made sure he knew of his inadequacy. It enraged him. In response, as Romero stresses, men like my father will create more financial problems to spite the SBW's takeover (in Jackson and Greene, 2000). My father is overwhelmingly guilty, a repeat offender, re-garding this. He never divulged any of his dealings. One just had to discover them later. Still, he gave no explanation. I heard my mother say once that he was threatened by the fact that she increasingly made more money than him. It's true. He was. In his shame, he maintained a great distance from his family. (If it is true that "African-American men are more likely than men of other ethnic groups to endorse traditional attitudes about masculinity" [Cour-tenay, 2004, p. 60], then we must consider the consequences of the Quixo-tean[2] impossibilities of the unachievable dream as it pertains to Black men and those who love them.) My father was a magician—focusing on misdirec-tion. He did anything to try and ensure that we would not see his lack of intellectual prowess and his lack of money. It was an awful experience to witness this man's life. He was obviously hurting but, in his coolness, he violated others. I don't know the myriad of ways in which he suffered be-cause we never spoke of this. But let me not use this as his excuse; for there is none. This cool of his, appeared most sadistic, most calculating, most deceptive. And a cool of this kind is the weed that destroys the harvest. For what woman can bear the seeds of a *cool* deception? What happens when she knows the magician's secrets?

Nevertheless, I wonder about the men who keep their partners at a dis-tance; who appear distant in family photographs; who keep the world at bay;

who avoid any collision or encounter with their storms. When in public, and away from my mother, my father became misleadingly alive. He became a charlatan or a "cool guy" that people seemed to enjoy. "How's it going, Carl?" Asked by a teller at the bank, the worker behind the deli-counter, or an older Black man from his past, he responded always, "Oh, just takin' it easy," as both parties would laugh. I wondered who this man was and what elicited this public performance. He never looked at me or interacted with me or the rest of the family in this way. Always, with my mother, he brought a destabilizing catatonic cool. Like the SBW, the CBM is intended to be a performance of survival. In public, my father exhibited a degree of cool pose. Majors and Billson (1992) describe the cool pose embraced by many a Black man to be "a creative strategy devised by African American males to counter the negative forces in their lives" (p. 105). The pose is that which finds its roots on the continent of Africa and emerges in this American context as a defensive mask, a shield of protection. ". . . Cool pose helps him achieve a stern, impersonal masculinity in the face of adversity. . . . He can appear on the stage of life as competent, in control, playing to a diversity of audiences with flair and uniqueness (Majors and Billson, 1992, p. 28).

Outside our home, my father presented a self that appeared immune to anyone and anything. He wore a mask "to defend against his fear of total disintegration and loss of self" (Majors and Billson, 1992, p. 61). This "cool pose" Majors and Billson (1992) write:

> Is potentially counterproductive when a man becomes obsessed with being cool just to win a woman's heart, only to find that the relationships sours when true intimacy does not materialize. He has become obsessed with being cool in order to obtain the rewards of courtship (sexual intimacy), but he fails to win genuine closeness and companionship because he has not allowed his deeper feelings to surface. (p. 44)

The mask helps to impede the display of vulnerability and hinder the touch of the oceanic depths. He would rather not travel to a vulnerable place. Endlessly he presents an anesthetized self deeply sedated by catatonic cool, which reinforces in him a sort of safe room. He may play a part in the public sphere, but behind closed doors he conceals his innermost rooms. I consider, how many boyfriends, husbands, fathers, are physically present yet emotionally absent? What does this do to those around him? I wonder about the men who hide from themselves, hide from their partners, evacuate life, disengage from any sort of "being-present" with others.

WHITENED COMPLICATIONS

Further complicating the multitude of dynamics at work between Diana and Carl, and what I see as that which exists between many a Black middle-class or mixed-class couple, is this: He remained endlessly bothered by Diana's refusal and inability to enter White womanhood. He believed his White patriarchal social position would be enlivened once she displayed the womanhood he demanded she find within her. To Carl, whiteness was not a destructive force between them.

Diana, on the other hand, unconsciously demanded her husband to enter, acceptably, a traditional White manhood that would "somehow" not adhere to White patriarchal elements—one that was—White manhood a la carte. She remained frustrated by his inability to garner the societal spoils, the socioeconomic riches and socioeconomic position, reflective of a version of White manhood. Diana's belief that she had been forced to play a role she viewed as a traditionally male one branded him as an antagonist.

In this, attempts to mirror White institutional gender roles and definitions fail at the onset. Utterances of be "the man" or "woman" are ripe with mandates for us to perpetuate unyieldingly destructive performances. What I am detailing is the Black male's struggle for a misleading manhood, one that manifests as a condemning force—for that which he often seeks, is forever illusive. For if the Black male believes in the manhood detailed by White males (as being the main provider, etc.) yet is not allowed access to the channels in which he may achieve or experience what can be described as Whitened manhood, internal tensions will arise. Carl clutched to his coolness in the face of this reality, and destruction abounded.

Looking backward, we must also acknowledge the impact of social messages on many a woman's formative years. In this, "society," Romero adds, "gave the SBW messages that love was associated with what she did and how she looked, not who she was" (Jackson and Greene, 2000, p. 230). Looking back, we must remember, in the wake of formal slavery, strength was that which "Black women could salvage about their personal identities." It was that which made them "infinitely stronger than the White women" (Walker-Barnes, 2014, pp. 93–94). To the White society, the Black woman was never feminine in the manner the White woman was/is (Beauboeuf-Lafontant, 2007, 2009).

CONCLUDING THOUGHTS

My father referred to his wife as "the old ball and chain," while my mother spent over a decade reminding her children of the "idiot" she wished she never married. As I grew older, I realized what happened to my parents: they collided with one another, in holy matrimony, while running desperately from the storms of their past and from the atmospheric turmoil within. Marriage did nothing to calm the storms which frightened them. Marriage can often breed more unrest. My parents dared not allow the other too close. It is true, storms stimulated by joy exist (Eigen, 2005), but Diana and Carl dared not linger, disturbed by monsters, real and imagined, in the depths of this feeling either. "People function," Eigen (1996) writes, "as filters for one another" (p. 195). I take this to convey the importance of allowing a patient reciprocity to emerge as we crash mightily into one another. We catch bits and pieces of what is psychically diffused by the other. Not everything goes through us. Yes, "We have an impact on each other and respond to another's impact. If we are lucky we let the other's impact play on us" (p. 195).

Unconsciously led by an ideology of mastery and dominance, a psychic imperialism emerges in which one overrepresents and wishes for their illusionary projections of self-mastery via strength and coolness, to colonize all psychic life, I worry about our "emotional lungs filled with psychospiritual mucous" and "undiagnosed emotional pneumonia;" and the "chronic emotional colds" (Eigen, 2005, p. 84). Racialized rhinopharyngitis lingers in our lives. Pigmentocratic kingdoms induce influenza. Eigen (2005) illuminates how the disturbances in one's life, in some general sense, impact one's emotional world. Consider this: What runs through the Black's life is often too overwhelming to bear. Cyclones brew. Soon, the tsunami of our racialized experiences crashes mightily onto our partner's shores.

NOTES

1. Biblical: Mark 5. Eigen (2005), *Emotional Storm*, emphasizes this point.
2. Reference to Don Quixote.

BIBLIOGRAPHY

Abrams, J. A., Hill, A., & Maxwell, M. (2018). Underneath the mask of the strong black woman schema: Disentangling influences of strength and self-silencing on depressive symptoms among us Black women. *Sex Roles: A Journal of Research*. https://doi.org/10.1007/s11199-018-0956-y

Beauboeuf-Lafontant, T. (2007). You Have to Show Strength: An Exploration of Gender, Race, and Depression. *Gender & Society*, 21(1), 28–51.

Beauboeuf-Lafontant, T. (2009). *Behind the Mask of the Strong Black Woman : Voice and the Embodiment of a Costly Performance*. Philadelphia: Temple University Press.

Bion, W. R. (1994/1979), Making the best of a bad job. In *Clinical Seminars and Other Works*. London: Routledge.

Brand, D. (2002). *A map to the door of no return: Notes to belonging*. Toronto: Vintage Canada.

Courtenay, W. H. (2004). Best practices for improving college men's health. *New Directions for Student Services*, 2004(107), 59–74.

Eigen, M. (1996). *Psychic deadness*. Northvale, NJ: Jason Aronson.

Eigen, M. (2005). *Emotional storm*. Middletown, CT: Wesleyan University Press.

Eigen, M., & Govrin, A. (2007). *Conversations with Michael Eigen*. London: Karnac.

Harris-Lacewell, M. (2001) No Place to Rest, *Women & Politics*, *23*(3), 1–33.

Majors, R., & Billson, J. M. (1992). *Cool pose: The dilemmas of Black manhood in America*. Lexington Books.

Nelson, T., Cardemil, E. V., & Adeoye, C. T. (2016). Rethinking Strength. *Psychology of Women Quarterly*, *40*(4), 551.

Romero, R. (2000). The Icon of the strong Black woman: The paradox of strength. In Jackson, L. C., & Greene, B. *Psychotherapy with African American women: Innovations in psychodynamic perspectives and practice* (pp. 225–238). New York: Guilford Press.

Sharpe, C. (2016). *In the Wake: On Blackness and Being*. Durham: Duke University Press.

Shorter-Gooden, K., Washington, N. C., Phinney, J. S., & Goossens, L. (1996). Young, Black, and female: the challenge of weaving an identity. *Identity Development in Context*, (5), 465.

Walker-Barnes, C. (2014). *Too heavy a yoke : black women and the burden of strength*. Eugene, OR : Cascade Books, 2014.

Walker-Barnes, C. (2017). When the Bough Breaks: The StrongBlackWoman and the Embodiment of Stress. In Evans, S. Y., Bell, K., & Burton, N. K. *Black Women's Mental Health: Balancing Strength and Vulnerability*, (pp. 43–55). Albany: SUNY Press.

Wilderson, F. B. (2010). *Red, white & black: Cinema and the structure of U.S. antagonisms*. Durham, NC: Duke University Press.

Woods-Giscombé, C. L. (2010). Superwoman Schema: African American Women's Views on Stress, Strength, and Health. *Qualitative Health Research*, *20*(5), 668–683.

Chapter Five

"What's Love Got to Do with It?" — A Piece for the Brothas

Evelyn Amponsah

Writing this piece was a difficult task for me. I knew what I wanted to write but could not write it. Words failed me because this topic that I endeavored to make intelligible is intimate and has been foreclosed to Black women. I struggled with the notion that I had to write this with the least amount of bias as possible. I wanted to write about interracial relationships and why they are important sites for critique and dialogue. I wanted to do this without being dismissed because of the negative view that only bitter and jealous Black women have "problems" with interracial relationships. This stance is one that has worked to silence the valid insights, critiques, and questions Black women have raised in relation to interracial relationships, and in fact, even within this space, where black love is privileged, it worked to silence me. Black women have and continue to be discounted as knowledge producers in romantic relationship because they have been relegated to a position of eternal singlehood where they raise abandoned children on their own, while presenting a strong maternal front against injustices wielded against them by deadbeat partners and lazy husbands. Yet, what most Black females know is that at one point or another they had to consider the idea that a Black male would not be interested in them because "he doesn't like Black girls." What I mean here is that even though, the way in which a certain type of interracial dating (one which privileges White/Latina/Asian women over Black women) affects the materiality of Black womanhood, we have been dismissed as experts of our own experience because "we are bitter."

Therefore, to circumvent this and to present myself as someone who should and can write about this, I tried to remove myself from the writing. I tried to legitimize this piece through theory, gathering quote after quote from theorists after theorists, gathering research and data to point to an experience I know to be true. Further, the bitter Black woman stereotype makes us vulnerable to attack by those who believe love, sex, and relationships are matters of the heart and cannot be controlled or politicized; that love, sex, and relationships are personal, private things, which must not be questioned; and that any Black woman who has something to say about an interracial relationship has nothing of value to contribute. The expectation is I will be attacked about the things I have to say here. Like the Black women before me who tried to write about this and like those after me will most likely suffer, I will face the dismissal as bitter, as jealous, and as angry. So, to cut short that unnecessary song and dance, I will state clearly and unequivocally that:

1. Am not bitter
2. My man has never been "stolen" by a White woman (Becky could never)
3. I am not jealous, neither am I a "hater" or whatever else people might say to dismiss the valid critiques Black women have in relation to this topic.

What I am, is interested in love, and yes this is a conversation about love. I am interested in having an important conversation about what it means to Black women when Black men—those who center blackness; who do the important work of theorizing Black existence; who take the time to unpack the denigration of blackness; who "big up" Black women in their public/ professional lives—choose to date, marry, and have sex with White women in their "private lives." I am one who joins bell hooks in "believing in love's promise," which "informs our decisions, strengthens our understanding of community [and] keeps us together" (1999, p. xxvii). Love tells us we are worthy and that is powerful. As one who believes "[that] sexuality [is] an anchoring point for the reproduction of relations of oppression, not only between colonizer and colonized, but among the colonized themselves" (Mercer, 1994, p. 124), I am interested in having this conversation. And because "[t]oday we believe in the possibility of love, and that is the reason why we are endeavoring to trace its imperfections and perversions" (Fanon, 2008, p. 24), I would like to confront this matter openly and intimately.

Like Fanon, I consider an interracial relationship as rooted in a conscious and/or unconscious need for Black people to gain White privilege or acceptance and as a perversion and an imperfection of love. I "think of love as a verb [because] it creates a sense of intention, action, responsibility (. . .) [because] if we believe in love as something that just happens to us, we don't feel responsible for it, we don't feel like we made it happen, or are an active participant in its growth, in its sustainability" (hooks, 1999, p. 12). Together hooks and Fanon allow me the space needed to critique interracial love as biased and to critique Black people as active participants in black love. We can be intentional about the power of love and about how we use love, especially when we know relationships reproduce power and powerlessness, yet remain unchecked.

Intimacy and love are the places where most of us seek our value. We want love from those we think deserve our love and we also want to be loved by someone we have deemed deserving to love us, this can also be considered a perversion of love, especially if we use the definition of love hooks (2001) borrows from Enrich Fromm: "the will to extend one's self for the purpose of nurturing one's own or another's spiritual growth" (p. 4). This definition follows the description of love in 1 Corinthians 13:4–8a from the New Testament:

> 4. Love is patient, love is kind. It does not envy, it does not boast, it is not proud. 5. It does not dishonor others, it is not self-seeking, it is not easily angered, it keeps no record of wrongs. 6. Love does not delight in evil but rejoices with the truth. 7. It always protects, always trusts, always hopes, always perseveres.

Most people would agree with these types of definitions of love, however most of us do not love in this way. In fact, "dictionary definitions tend to define love as a profoundly tender, passionate affection for another person, especially when based on sexual attraction" (hooks, 1999, p. 3). What this tells us is that the investments we have in love are indeed selfish and are indeed imperfections and perversions. The definition of love posited by hooks, Fromm, and in the Bible are extremely important to this conversation as they bring us all to the same starting point and answer Tina Turner's famous question *What's love got to do with it*? This article posits and works through the reasons why sexual politics and practices of Black radical thinkers, Black social commenters, and Black activists are necessary sites of investigation within the Black Radical Tradition (BRT), I suggest that those of us who are invested in and understand the ways in which white supremacy, whiteness and anti-blackness structure our lives should be choosing Black people as lovers, and romantic partners because of the power of black love. To do this work, this article organizes around four major arguments,

1. The Hegelian notion of Recognition—both through Hegel and Fanon.
2. Why Black women care and why any Black person should care?
3. The centering of whiteness and/or investments in whiteness
4. Accountability to encourage a more nuanced dialogue about desire, recognition, and value in the sexual practices and politics of Black Radical Thinkers/social activists.

"YOU DON'T KNOW MY NAME" — ALICIA KEYS

Mistakenly, feelings are the thing that most people want to be impartial and uncontrollable. "You can't help who you fall in love with" is a statement many might consider true. However, I argue, who we "feel" for is a question of the "struggle for recognition" as theorized by Hegel and colleagues in *the Phenomenology of Spirit* (1979). Very, and I mean *very* simply put, the struggle for *recognition* is the need for two self-conscious beings to recognize the other as self-consciousness. For Hegel, self-consciousness is the ability to recognize oneself as a being, an individual, separate from the environment, who has their own will. This requires that one recognizes they are self-conscious, and that somehow, they recognize the other as also self-conscious to validate their self-consciousness. The important part of recognition for Hegel is that one can only recognize one's self-consciousness if another self-conscious being recognizes one's consciousness. Loving someone and wanting them to love you back or wanting someone and wanting them to want you back is a fundamental struggle for recognition. We do not say "I love you" without the expectation of having it affirmed and reciprocated. Indeed, if one says those words, it is because they have determined that person is worthy of their love and that person will in turn say "I love you, too," confirming their worth. It is through the other's worthiness that one's own worth is affirmed and recognized.

I call this the "You Don't Know My Name" phenomenon. In this song, Alicia Keys says, there is something special about the other person, therefore she wants him to know her name (to know her) because others are not worth her time. So, this person whom she does not know, she has already deemed to be worthy of knowing her name based on the value that is attributed to what she deems as their "specialness." This special one is worth her time and must know her name so that she too can feel validated and worthy. Keys does not simply want the other to know her name, but she wants him to *know* her name—intimately. Her lyrics emphasize the importance of the personal realm as a site that reproduces values that align people based on the recognition of their names (cultural, sexual, gender, politics, etc.). Names, as cultural capital, can be used to bring together into personal spaces or to marginalize others based on their "lack of" sociopolitical value.

French Sociologist Pierre Bourdieu argues that cultural capital is the foundation of social life and dictates one's position within the social order. Extending beyond the economic it encapsulates symbolic elements such as skills, tastes, posture, clothing, mannerisms, material belonging, credentials and other factors one acquires by belonging to a social class. Bourdieu's analysis of the various forms of capital is in relation to social class, however, we can also think about the various forms of capital and how they are impacted by race. I would argue that race is a cultural capital commodity. More specifically, anti-blackness privileges everything white over everything black, including White women. This would mean that most people understand that whiteness has a certain value and the closer in proximity you are to whiteness, the more value you gain/have. In the colonial context, and through the process of colonization, whiteness is a prized possession in comparison to blackness. It is valued in comparison to blackness, therefore, one might conclude that when we seek love from White people it is because we have deemed either on a conscious or unconscious level that whiteness is more valuable than blackness and to be worthy of and receive white love is more meaningful, than to receive black love.

So, Jamal might value Meghan Radcliffe over T'Keisha Thomas or Adjoa Amoabeng because he perceives one as a way forward socially and the other as holding him back. Of this Fanon states, "[m]y beloved will support me energetically in assuming my virility whereas the need to earn the admiration or love of others will weave a valorizing web over my vision of the world" (2008, p. 24). Fanon also says,

> out of the Blackest part of my soul, through the zone of hachures, surges up this desire to be suddenly white. I want to be recognized not as Black but as White. (. . .) who better than the white woman to bring this about? By loving me, she proves to me that I am worthy of white love. I am loved like a white man. I am a white man. Her love opens the illustrious path that leads to total fulfillment (Fanon, 2008, p. 45).

Fanon is telling us that love is a form of recognition. One way for Black people to enter whiteness is through being wanted/loved by white people. For a White person to want to love you means they have recognized you, they see you, they know your name, they know your value. While this interaction between two self-conscious beings appears to be happening in isolation, we must be aware that the white supremacist system and the wider social system is a part of the interracial dynamic. In *Black Skin, White Masks* (2008), Frantz Fanon notes "[w]hen my restless hands caress those white breasts, they grasp white civilization and dignity and make them mine. I marry white culture, white beauty, white whiteness" (p. 45). Fanon, who was married to a White woman, is among numerous Black male thinkers/influencers, activists, social justice warriors (e.g., CLR James and Donald Glover) who have White partners. Fanon is interested in desire and the ways in which those whom we desire and those who desire us in return reaffirm our value. By extension of that White woman's love, Fanon sees himself ingratiated within the white system that has long shut out Black people. The White woman enters blackness by proxy and further sees herself as absolved from the racism of whiteness because her man is black. However, several questions arise out of these struggles and desires for recognition: Do they understand this struggle for recognition in relation to their own self-consciousness? What are they self-conscious about? Since recognition becomes or is equal to value, if a third person (say a Black woman) who is self-conscious is introduced to their space, does it alter their value?

I suggest that it is critical we ask these questions, specifically in relation to Black men who champion blackness politically, yet in their personal lives, do not date Black women. If on an intellectual and political level, these men, like Fanon, understand that whiteness is valued over blackness and therefore, White women are valued over Black women, then these men should understand that their interactions with White women reaffirm the sociopolitical value of White women over Black women. This is the thing that Black women understand and know too well; Black men's interactions with White women speak to the positionality of Black women. Black women and White women exist in a dialectical relationship.

"HE BETTER CALL BECKY WITH THE GOOD HAIR"—BEYONCÉ

Something interesting happened that annoyed a lot of Black women in 2017. Actor and activist Jesse Williams was rumored to have divorced his Black wife of thirteen years and was dating . . . wait for it . . . a white woman! Black women were past annoyed! Because, in 2016, during an acceptance speech for the humanitarian award on BET, Jesse Williams fixed his mouth to say "[t]his is also in particular . . . for the Black women in particular, who have spent their lifetimes dedicated to nurturing everyone before themselves. We can and will do better for you." This statement almost became laughable when within the next few months, rumors of Williams dating "Becky with the good hair" started circulating. Black women on social media and beyond started asking valid questions, attempting to hold this man accountable for his words. When he said, "we can and will do better for you," what exactly did he mean? Was this relationship with a White woman the "do better?" Not surprisingly, these critiques were met with, *Why does it matter who he dates? Y'all are just jealous and bitter.*

My Brotha, dismissing Black women's valid questions and critiques because you do not have answers for us requires some serious introspection that you may not be ready for. We, Black women know it's difficult but look to Fanon (2008) for an example in *Black Skin, White Masks*, where he interrogates the relationship of the Black woman and the White man, postulating among other things that "she is seen as participating in racial suicide through her attempt to engage in a sexual relationship with a White man" (Young, 1996, p. 89). I mean, why is the racially suicidal White woman more valuable to you than the Black woman who as Jesse Williams said nurtures everyone above herself? We get it. "Black male sexual acts with white women, constitute an initiation, a Black male/rite/right of passage into masculinity-conquering and debasing the white man's possession—rather than simply a betrayal of race" (Young, 1996, p. 94) but do you consider what is really at stake?

Y'all are hypocrites! Before you lash out at me let's refer to Fanon (2008) who does not have the same analysis of interracial relationship when it comes to Black men and White women versus Black women and White men. Rather than be held accountable and interrogate your positions and decisions to engage in any kind of conversation with us, it is easier to dismiss us as bitter. To repeat, my focus here is not on just any Black man. I am talking to you "woke" brotha's saying loud you're Black and proud but panting white names in the heat of the night with the lights on, so you can see all of the white . . .

I am specifically concerned with the Black men who have a politics of blackness; the ones who claim to love and support Black women; the ones who claim to understand what it means to be a Black women in a world that devalues us; the ones who use Black womanhood to enhance their careers (e.g., Jesse Williams's Black female fan base grew drastically after his BET speech); the ones who should know that by dating White women (whether they like it or not), they invest in and promote the notions that Black women are unworthy of love where White women are; and finally, to the ones who claim to love Black women but then don't *love* Black women. How can a Black woman not be bitter when the man who claims to know and understand her turns around and gives his love to a system that has stamped her down and degraded her repeatedly?

Here, I'd like to return to the title of this section to help us think about what this bitterness and annoyance is about. When Beyoncé states "he better call Becky with the good hair," she is highlighting two things:

1. She emphasizes the typically White name "Becky" over her own Black name Beyoncé.
2. She criticizes the view that European-type hair and other bleached standards of beauty are better than Afrocentric beauty.

Call Becky with the good hair if that's what you want. Go have her and miss me with that bullshit—justifying your white preferences by claiming I am not feminine enough; submissive enough; I am too dominate, too angry, too argumentative, too much; and I'm too prudish to let you explore your sexual freedom the way a White woman would. If you take the time to question your desire for a White woman you might see that you value and crave the White woman's recognition because of your conscious or unconscious investment in whiteness. Even when you stand up and denounce white supremacy, racism, and oppression, there is something in you that wants the power those systems give. So, you will lash out at me, the Black woman, humiliate me and stamp me down, dismiss me and accuse me of not being enough because you feel your own lack. "No! No! Hell nah!" (Beyoncé).

"WHAT HAVE YOU DONE FOR ME LATELY?"—JANET JACKSON

Will and choice are a central part of the conversation. If as hook's suggests—and I do agree—we choose to love, what does it mean for us that the men, who "should" choose Black women, do not? Misogynoir is a form of misogyny that centralizes on race, particularly positioning Black women in a very unique place where the experience of racism from other races is compounded by misogyny from men. Though Black men may invest in anti-blackness, they may not invest in dismantling misogynoir because as men, they benefit from this system of patriarchy that affords them sociocultural and political dominance over Black women. Black men, particularly the "woke" kind may not admit their investment in misogynoir as they must self-interrogate the ways in which they are invested in a value system that devalues the blackness contained in women in multiple ways. They would also have to reckon with the possibility that their desire for an interracial relationship can and will center the comfort of White women (their partner) and whiteness. Meaning, they will do things (even anti-Black things) for the sake and comfort of their partners because this person is their partner and they are invested in their feelings.

This split desire presents an entanglement with the social and the political within Black Radical Thought/Black Studies and the BRT. If on an intellectual level, one understands how the denigration of blackness functions, how then on a personal level can one make the choice to participate in it, especially, if you consider yourself a "woke" individual. As a Black woman, I expect that what these men are saying to be reflected in what these men are demonstrating romantically. Are they practicing what they preach or are they drinking the Kool-aid between sermons? How can they believe Black is beautiful but follow the white supremacist ascribed standards of beauty and give their most intimate selves to whiteness? My brotha, "we all have to look at what and who we bring to bed with us every night because they deeply inform the thinking, living and working we do beyond closed doors" (Uwujaren, 2017, p. 5).

In conclusion, "The word "love" is most often defined as a noun, yet all the more astute theorists of love acknowledge that we would all love better if we used it as a verb" (hooks, 1999, p. 4). Recently, it was revealed that Tupac made the choice to stop dating Madonna because as he wrote "I would be letting down half of the people who made me what I thought I was." This decision by Tupac juxtaposed with Jesse Williams's embracing Becky's cuteness captures the exact conversation we've just shared. I want to think about love as a verb and how we can all make conscious decisions to love, specifically Black women. Much of what has been written here can and should be debated. But if we cannot move to this space of intimacy to think about how power and oppression are reproduced then what we do in the public realm might as well mean nothing. More explicitly, if, My Brotha, you can only love Black women in the public gaze, through political and intellectual endeavors, and not in the so called private sphere then you are not choosing us, not reaffirming our value and not extending yourself for the purpose of growth, which undermines any public statement you can make about the Black woman. If you and I are committed to the uplifting of Black people, then you and I should be committed to each other; this cannot be a purely intellectual task. hooks (1996) notes "[d]ialogue makes love possible. I want to think critically about intellectual partnership, about the ways Black women and men resist by creating a world where we can talk with one another where we can work together" (p. 80). My Brotha, take this call to action seriously. If you believe in love's promise, that love matters, if your politics are about blackness, you must choose a Black woman not only for intellectual partnership but also to bring to bed every night and dream.

REFERENCES

Fanon, F. (2008). *Black Skin, White Masks*. New York: Grove Press.
Harris, J., & Jackson, J. (1986). "What Have You Done for Me Lately?" [Jackson, J]. On *Control*. Flyte Tyme Studios. Minneapolis, Minnesota (1985).
Hegel, G. W. F., A. V. Miller, J. N. Findlay, & J. Hoffmeister. (1979). *Phenomenology of Spirit*. Oxford, England: Clarendon Press.
hooks, b. (1999). *All about Love: New Visions*. New York: William Morrow.
hooks, b. (1996). "Feminism as a Persistent Critique of History: What's Love Got to Do with It?" in *The Fact of Blackness: Frantz Fanon and Visual Representation*. Seattle: Bay Press.
Keys, A., & West, K., (2003). "You Don't Know My Name." [Keys, A]. On *The Diary of Alicia Keys*, RCA/Jive, [MP3]. New York City (2002).
Knowles-Carter, B., Rhoden, S., & Wynter, G. (2016). "Sorry." [Knowles-Carter]. On *Lemonade*. Los Angeles: Parkwood/Columbia, [MP3].
Mercer, K. (1994). *Welcome to the Jungle: New Positions in Black Cultural Studies*. New York: Routledge.
Uwujaren, J. (2017, June 8). "Can I Date a White Person and Still Be Woke" is the wrong question. Retrieved from https://racebaitr.com/2017/06/08/can-date-white-person-still-woke-wrong-question/
Young, Lola. (1996). "Missing Persons: Fantasising Black Women in Black Skin, White Masks" in *The Fact of Blackness: Frantz Fanon and Visual Representation*. Seattle: Bay Press.

Chapter Six

No Longer "Obsolete" and "Dangerous," but Still Single

Black Masculinity and Marriage in African American Film at the Dawn of the Twenty-First Century

Riché Richardson

Whether public dialogues have been ameliorative and well-intentioned or just plain stereotypical, "crisis" has been an operative term in relation to Black men. It seems somewhat inevitable that the notion of crisis has also underwritten some popular representations of Black men. In film, perhaps no single moment heralded more compellingly and graphically the perceived crisis of black masculinity that would come to preoccupy the genre during the early 1990s than the depiction of the brutal slaying of the character Ricky as portrayed by Morris Chestnut in the director John Singleton's 1991 film *Boyz n the Hood.* This was just one film among a range of others, including *Straight Outta Brooklyn* (1991), *Sugar Hill* (1993), *Menace II Society* (1993), *New Jack City* (1991), *Dead Presidents* (1995), and *Juice* (1992), that grappled thematically with the violence and devastation that gangs, guns, and drugs have wrought in urban and predominantly black communities in the United States during the postindustrial, post–civil rights era.

I first saw *Boyz n the Hood* as a new release with a group of my peers while studying as an undergraduate in an interdisciplinary summer program at Boston University. Even now, I can vividly remember how inconsolably we cried that afternoon in the theater when we saw Ricky gunned down and his dream of going on to college on a football scholarship forever deferred. It is undeniable that this film, and this image in particular, shocked us and moved us. I heard legitimate criticisms of the problematic masculinism of *Boyz n the Hood* in the months thereafter, including an assertive critique of the film's patriarchal dimension by bell hooks at the Atlanta University Center's Woodruff Library once I returned to Spelman that fall. I had the opportunity to interview John Singleton myself as associate editor of the newspaper alongside men from Morehouse as he visited the latter campus during homecoming. In the group interview I raised my own concerns to him about the scene in which Brandi (Nia Long) finally sleeps with Tre (Cuba Gooding, Jr.) and loses her virginity to him after his traumatic encounter with the police, which to me seemed to prioritize his pain over her own personal values and boundaries that she had made clear in the past.

Yet, this dominant narrative depicting Black men as victims of violence in African American film obscured other contemporaneous crises of black masculinity. For instance, the silent and unseen deaths of many Black gay men from AIDS should have evoked the sympathies and concerns in the African American context that we related to the graphic and violent death of Ricky. The formulation of Black men as an "endangered species" in public and popular dialogues, notwithstanding the limits of this term, might have been much more complex had it encompassed other issues to complement the dialogues on the precarious condition of young urban Black men. Perhaps more than anyone in the African American context, Haki Madhubuti, formerly known as the Black Arts Movement poet Don Lee, helped to popularize the idea of Black men as an "endangered species" in *Black Men: Obsolete, Single, Dangerous?* (Madhubuti, 1989).

I noticed another genre when my mother gave me the video for *The Best Man* and encouraged me to watch it, around age thirty, likely to encourage me to think more about men of my own age and to remind me that they were out there, given my isolation in the ivory tower working toward tenure, and to encourage me to think of marriage in a more open-minded way beyond my narrow hope to marry another professor. That one of my closest girlfriends, Denise, who was working as an assistant professor in Florida, watched *The Best Man* frequently, enjoyed its wedding themes, and said that it was her favorite film, also piqued my interest. But as much as I tried to enjoy it and like it, my reaction to the film was still a bit more lukewarm than hers. Still, *The Best Man* was the lens through which I began to take note of the small body of African American film that centered a Black male cast and focused on themes related to love, relationships, and marriage, and that I will discuss here. That it is now a veritable classic and has a sequel featuring its original cast entitled *The Best Man Holiday* (2013) also underscores its significance in the body of African American film and as a site on which to reflect on relationships, which also points to the value of critical reflection on it, as well as related films.

This is a discussion to which I come as a scholar who works in areas such as Black feminism, cultural studies, film studies and Black/Africana studies. I also come to it as a woman who has long been fascinated by the topic of relationships, who came of age with the generation of Black young adults represented in the films that I discuss, and who found some of their messages to be deeply disturbing once I took a look at them and thought about them. Because they recurrently focus primarily on issues related to Black men, marriage, and relationships, a critical examination of these cinematic works, is useful, I suggest, not only for pondering problems in representing Black men and women in film, including persisting stereotypes of race, gender, class, and sexuality, but also for analyzing complications related to marriage, dating, and relating for Black men and women.

W. E. B. Du Bois's formulation of "double consciousness" in feelings of alienation for being both Black and American suggested, quite well, the utility of methods for using psychology as a lens for examining African Americans and the issue of their otherness in the United States at the outset of the twentieth century. The almost taboo status that topics related to mental health occupy among African Americans is well known. The chasm between psychoanalysis and race has been an issue of frustration in academia among critics who remain invested in the field, and work to address the elisions of race within psychoanalysis has been sustained in the repertoires of a range of critics (Spillers, 2003; Tate, 1998; Lane, 1998; Cheng, 2001). On the other hand, there has been much dialogue at the "grassroots" level in the African American context surrounding matters of mind and the urgent need for black psychological recovery, an issue that is usually rhetorically pronounced in relation to the residual scars of slavery and ongoing victimization within a white supremacist culture that breeds self-hatred among Blacks, aesthetically and otherwise. Madhubuti's study is but one of a booming economy of texts that reveal this preoccupation with the topic of psychology. Such books, whose scholarly methods are frequently inflected by Black Nationalist ideology, continued to have widespread currency in African American bookstores toward the end of the twentieth century. A preoccupation with psychological matters is similarly evident in the body of black film released around the turn of the millennium that recurrently focused on themes related to Black male friendships, relationships, and marriage, which aspects of my discussion will reveal.

Representations of Black men in films of the early 1990s were complemented by the media fascination with gangsta rap focused on crime and violence, from which I am tracing an intriguing shift in Black masculine representations toward an emphasis on Black male interiority. This thematic trajectory concomitantly emphasized the topic of Black male-female relationships, including issues related to marriage. For instance, in the 2001 film *The Brothers*, the character Jackson, who is portrayed by Morris Chestnut, is featured in the opening sequence sitting on his therapist's couch and dialoging about his anxieties concerning marriage and commitment. He discovers later in the film that his love interest has been dating his father. Similarly,

Lance, the character portrayed by Chestnut in the film *The Best Man*, discovers that his fiancé has previously dated his best friend, the best man, at the wedding. These circumstances are tortuous for the leading men and are salient in developing the plots of both films. More generally, these films, to which others such as *The Wood* and *Head of State* were also fitting complements, were invested in interrogating the challenges of negotiating endogamous heterosexual love relationships for thirty-year-old professional Black men. In these instances, the crisis of urban violence that was so salient in African American film of the early 1990s was replaced by crises of friendships, love relationships, family, and mental health.

It intrigues me that Morris Chestnut journeyed from death on the street as Ricky in *Boyz n the Hood* to the therapist's couch as a suited, professional, and highly articulate member of the Black middle class in *The Brothers*. Indeed, we might interpret his evolution as a marker of a transition in Black masculine representation in African American film. Whatever other concerns are manifest, anxieties surrounding marriage and commitment are salient in all of these films. Through various strategies, all stage marriage ceremonies, perhaps manifesting what Elizabeth Freeman has described, concerning film in general, as "a national wedding complex in the psychoanalytic sense, America's terrible case of heterosexual exhibitionism, or . . . its mass fixation on the primal scene of induction into that most intimate relationship, the married couple" (Freeman, 2002, pp. 1–2). In this vein, they also seem to grapple with African American social dating and marriage. In the period during which these films were released, the marriage rate in Black communities was estimated at 30 percent, nearly half of what its rate of 61 percent had been in 1960. According to statistics released in 2002 by the Centers for Disease Control and Prevention, Black women in this nation are the least likely women to get married, the most likely to be divorced, the least likely to remarry if they divorce and the oldest brides. Such statistics have not only served as a basis for representing marriage as being in crisis for Black women, but also for thinking about issues that have impacted the population demography and marriage rates of Black men in the United States, such as the system of mass incarceration, unemployment, educational opportunities, and homicide. Indeed, by the end of the twentieth century, the state of marriage for African Americans was often enunciated *as* a crisis. As these films illustrate, in some instances, crises related to Black masculinity and marriage were represented as being mutually constitutive. Platforms on family values, same-sex relations, and welfare reform developed by the neoconservative Republican right wing were the backdrop against which the public debate about the issue of marriage in the African American context unfolded.

Public and political dialogues on marriage, masculinity, and family reached their height during the 1990s in the Washington, D.C., Million Man March sponsored by Louis Farrakhan and the Nation of Islam. The aspect of this organization's agenda for the march that condemned welfare was the most salient indicator of the social conservatism that almost inevitably underpins such platforms and revealed the difficulty of constructing an alternative and progressive discourse on concepts such as marriage and family in the African American context. At the same time, the march challenged dominant narratives within the national arena that insistently script Black masculinity and Black femininity as deviant. Conservative welfare policies on marriage have sometimes condescendingly suggested that love, intimacy, work, and commitment are values that Black men just don't understand and must be taught, often reinforcing the view of Black masculinity as pathological while flagrantly ignoring factors such as the impact of the economy on marriage trends among Blacks, and while also excluding Black men who might be categorized as middle class altogether. That the spate of films in this genre was produced within a growing climate of neoconservatism on marriage and family in the nation invites reflection on the extent to which they reflect reactionary ideologies.

Ann duCille reminds us in her revealing study entitled *The Coupling Convention: Sex, Text, and Tradition in Black Women's Fiction* that "marriage . . . is not a transhistorical bourgeois ideal or a linear literary convention but a sign of the times that shifts with the times, the place, and the people. It takes on different social and political meanings for different historical subjects at different historical moments" (DuCille, 1993, p. 4). Her analysis reveals that the theme of marriage has been salient and sustained in African American women's literary texts. The acknowledgment of its meanings shifting provokes further consideration on how and why marriage has surfaced so assertively in films of the millennial era, and particularly within a body of film that focuses on African American *male* identity. For if marriage is indeed fundamentally a bourgeois institution, its status as a motif across a range of contemporary African American films provides a useful terrain on which to reflect on the intersection of class, race, gender, and sexuality in constructing Black masculinity.

It is significant that most of these films highlight the challenges of being Black, male, and middle class in relation to the theme of marriage. In this essay, I am particularly interested in highlighting the common ground that these films share where they construe middle-class models of Black femininity as being hostile to Black masculine subject formation, and eventually as being expendable and undesirable. Some seem ideologically loaded: educated, Black middle-class professional women are demonized while Black working-class women are romanticized as ideal mates. In almost every case, the rationale is evident at some level that happiness and success for a Black professional man resides in dumping the middle-class "bitch" he's with to pursue a love relationship with a less demanding, less ambitious, less pretentious "down-to-earth" Black woman who is understanding and easier to get along with, or "upgrading" into an interracial coupling. This logic is particularly fascinating as it recuperates, albeit in a feminine guise, the rhetoric of realness and authenticity often infused by class stereotyping and recasts "street" credibility (i.e., the notion of cool) as a priority in defining Black masculinity. Some of these films are infused, then, by class contestations of major proportions at various levels, and turn on their own version of the "high" and "low" while suggesting the need for more extensive and complex critical understanding of class in the African American context. They are not only fascinating to consider for highlighting anxieties among Black males concerning middle-class Black women, but also for their recurrent depiction of Black women as stalking brides. In this sense, I want to suggest that they draw on established formulas in mainstream cinema that show the preying woman stalking a helpless male, a genre punctuated by what Emily Fox Kales identifies as "backlash" productions such as *Fatal Attraction* that were "a popular cultural response to changes in women's economic and political status" (Kales, 2004, pp. 1631–37).

A HEADACHE FOR THE HEAD OF STATE: THE PSYCHOTIC WOMAN

Head of State, the 2003 film directed, produced and cowritten by the actor/comedian Chris Rock, features Chris Rock in the starring role of Alderman Mays Gilliam in Washington, D.C., whose jilting by his scolding, insensitive fiancée frustrated with his lack of money is the first of a chain of negative events toward the beginning of the film. As she prepares to move out, she throws back his engagement ring, hysterically proclaims her desire for a house, children, and vacations; tells him that he should act like a grown man for a change; be a real politician, "play the game" and "wear a suit"; that he is awful in bed; and expresses delight that a lapsed payment has resulted in the repossession of his car. After being evicted from his office and seeing a bus run over his bicycle, he spots her with another man. He can only chew on the bitter irony of being deserted when he needs her most to stand by his side. The joke is very much on this ex-fiancée, however, when by a twist of fate, Mays becomes a nationally prominent politician and becomes president of the United States. She, in turn, becomes increasingly desperate and obnoxious in her effort to win him back, harassing and stalking him. Her minor role becomes a running joke. Her appearance in a wedding gown and delusional reminders of their "engagement" suggests her utter insanity and gall. The poetic justice is that she can't have him, for he has found Lisa, a more understanding, down-to-earth working-class woman.

Portrayed by the actress Robin Givens, the casting of the fiancée was likely no accident and plays effectively on the stories that surfaced during the

1980s when she was best known as a Syracuse University graduate starring on the hit series *Head of the Class*. In the wake of her marriage to the boxer Mike Tyson, then a multimillionaire and heavyweight champion of the world, Givens was portrayed in both tabloids and some mainstream media as a controlling "gold-digger" who was manipulating the comparatively naive Tyson, whom she had married for his money. This popular representation of Givens reached its height in the wake of the couple's interview with the reporter Barbara Walters in 1988 in which Tyson appeared sedated. Indeed, this was a popular representation that entailed a scripting of Tyson as a "victim," an image with which the public empathized and that the tabloids freely propagated until Tyson became so infamously associated with abuses such as rape and domestic violence during the 1990s. The representation of Givens also builds upon her characterization as Jacqueline, the ambitious, conniving businesswoman in the 1992 film *Boomerang* with whom Marcus, portrayed by Eddie Murphy, is initially enamored. Givens also brought this stereotype to life by portraying a woman who outwits a self-avowed player and beats him at his own game; incidentally, a young Chris Rock appears as a mail carrier. This is a boomerang effect that is writ large for Mays's girl-friend, who even desperately pursues and stalks him from her hospital bed after she has been seriously injured while attempting to make contact with him.

We see Lisa at the beginning of the film working as a clerk in Mays's neighborhood filling station. The film primarily develops its larger theme related to authenticity through her. Ignoring his advisors telling him to avoid talking to "the help," Mays pulls her to the dance floor as she serves food during his first major campaign party. It is noteworthy that he wins her approval and friendship by playing the role of MC and encouraging attendees to do the electric slide, in effect turning the party into a less formal and stilted event to which she can relate. She surfaces as a strong supporter and is presented as the "future first wife" at the inaugural ball, symbolically dressed in white. They represent the American family of the future. As he increasing-ly wears hip-hop clothing and highlights its iconography in his campaign, the film illustrates his evolution into someone bold enough to be his own man and speak "from the heart," and who is a "real American." The representa-tion of the nation's first couple as Black is amazingly prescient in hindsight, for Barack Obama made history when he was elected as the nation's first Black president a few years later, as his wife, Michelle Obama, became the nation's first Black First Lady.

The film uses Black masculinity to deconstruct what Dana Nelson ana-lyzes as an elitist, White-centered model of the presidency, an agenda visual-ly manifest in the insertion of Mays's sculptural likeness into Mount Rush-more replete with a diamond earring (Nelson, 1998, pp. 204–205). The film also attempts to examine the compatibility of African American identity with

American citizenship. But a problem is that it ironically reinforces narratives about "real" blackness and real masculinity as much as it critiques conventional elitist, White-centered images of the "real American," a critique signaled in Mays's slang, trendy clothing, and love of Lisa, rejecting middle-class upward mobility.

Class is elemental to the film's construction of authentic blackness. Implicitly, to be a real Black and a real man, he must align himself with "street" iconography. This reinforces a narrow representational spectrum of blackness and masculinity, which is particularly problematic when many Blacks in the "real" social world frequently assume that becoming educated and speaking standard English amount to "acting White." The film's uncompromising instating of hip-hop *as* blackness in critiquing respectability reinforces this essentialist model of African American selfhood.

While punishing the "gold digger," Lisa is put on a pedestal and deemed fit to share the fruits of his hard work and climb up the ladder of political success alongside him. Indeed, because Lisa's role is largely ornamental, and she plays no active role other than reminding him to "run his race," she is implicitly rescued and offered a better life. This heroic aspect is explicit at the beginning of the film when Mays saves a senior woman and her cat from a burning house, which puts him in the limelight. Miserably as the film began, Mays' newfound love and happiness make him as triumphant personally as he is politically. The message of the film is that a less educated working-class woman is a better mate for a successful man, compared to the demanding, ambitious middle-class type embodied by Robin Givens. Lisa is both more likely to stand by her man and know her place.

Notwithstanding my observation of the portrayal of middle-class Black women as deviant and psychotic and of a working-class Black woman as romantic and encouraging of a more authentic Black masculinity, *Head of State* presents a few more redeeming qualities that are worth noting. Evoking productions such as *Primary Colors* (1996) and *Bullworth* (1998), *Head of State* makes a profound commentary by foregrounding two African Americans in shaping a discourse of family within the national arena, a coupling that is iterated in Mays's choice of his plain speaking, no nonsense brother as his running mate to complement the excessiveness and provocation of his own Black body in the theater of American politics at such a high level. Such representations disrupt by implication the right-wing ideologies of family values centered on a monolithic whiteness. *Head of State* also provided one of the most assertive engagements of the complex positioning of African Americans in the wake of the September 11 tragedy and the War on Iraq, particularly when it alludes to the isolationist rhetoric for the United States in the global context and attempts to encourage inclusiveness by replacing the rhetorical phrase of Mays's presidential opponent, "God Bless America and no place else," with "God Bless the World." Furthermore,

Mays's campaign speech about cleaning staff employed at hotels that they cannot afford to stay at or employees at malls where they cannot afford to shop attacks the condition of the labor force at the heart of modern economies, a hierarchy that he also attempts to subvert in his embrace of Lisa.

Indeed, Chris Rock's *Head of State* is an assertive and courageous activist statement from a director, which is perhaps all the more significant and stunning given Rock's more conservative comic posturing that entailed treatment of controversial issues in the African American context, strategies that helped to bring him fame early in his career. Perhaps the film's most provocative and hilarious moment occurs in the scene when the media leaks the speculation that America is about to have its first Black president in Mays. The camera zones in on a serene, monolithically beige suburban neighborhood in California, the last state where the precincts are still open, and moments later, Whites begin pouring into the streets, running to the polls for their lives to prevent this historic moment; the irony and surprise, however, is that they vote in favor of the Black candidate, speaking to Mays's crossover, cross-racial appeal, and anticipating the real-world success and appeal of contemporary young Black male politicians such as Barack Obama.

Those who have attempted to control how Mays dresses and talks, and to otherwise manipulate him include Deborah, his main Black woman political advisor portrayed by Lynn Whitfield. She refers to him once as an "ignorant ass nigger" and is thrown off the campaign bus as a result but because she finally supports his efforts to win the election in his way, she is not discredited in the vein of the Givens character. Deborah is the potentially betraying Black woman who sells the Black man out to White men, in a desperate effort to secure her ubiquitous presence as an African American woman in elite political circles. Mays's efforts to avoid the clutches of a manipulative, untrustworthy type of woman in his personal life are part of his struggle to reclaim his life and agency as a politician. Mays's setup as a candidate in the presidential election so that he will lose is the result of underhanded tinkering and manipulation, on par with what occurs in the 1985 film *Trading Places* when two wealthy corporate elites make a one-dollar bet to observe the impact of environment on morality by giving a homeless petty thief portrayed by Eddie Murphy a wealthy lifestyle. That Deborah is a successful Black woman who finally *does* do the right thing, however, sends the message, ever so subtly, that there are times when successful Black women may be trustworthy, but only if they submit to the Black man's vision.

THE BROTHERS AND THE STALKING BRIDES

If the image of the psychotic stalking bride is a peripheral aspect of *Head of State*, it takes center stage in the 2001 film *The Brothers* and becomes a symbol of deep-seated psychological fears of marriage and commitment. In this film, four young professional Black male characters—Jackson, Terry, Brian, and Derek—are friends who struggle with finding the best strategies to achieve love and happiness. Marriage is particularly wished for by Jackson, who is a successful doctor. Yet, in the opening scene, he dreams of white fabric, red roses, and a gun flash, images that reflect his view of commitment *as* death and his fear of marriage. Throughout the film, the specter of a bride with a gun haunts him and later materializes in Bebe, the fiancée of his friend Terry. Angrily seeking answers about why Terry chose to call off the wedding, Bebe shows up dressed in her gown and fires at Brian, Terry, and Jackson as they are barricaded in Brian's house. One of Jackson's greatest fears is to be like his father, a man he regards as arrogant and selfish, and who never treated a woman right.

As Emily Fox Kales has pointed out,

> backlash films depict women who either through sexual seduction or professional power seek to dominate and destroy a male protagonist by their drive to possess, devour or annihilate him . . . Hollywood mainstream cinema for the most part produced and directed by males . . . are projections of male anxiety about their 'castration' and loss of potency—i.e., loss of exclusive dominance and entitlement in the workplace, the bedroom, the military and other institutional domains. As such, these films represent a form of cultural myth-making which seeks to regain a sense of control over the social forces threatening patriarchal order and stability. (Kales, 2003, pp. 1631–32)

Kales goes on to remark that "The myth in these backlash films is embodied in the cinematic image of the female predator, who represents the monstrous or murderous nature of feminine power, and the social message behind the myth is that women who have large appetites for competition, exertion of will and assertion of their own needs must indeed be monsters—unnatural, grotesque, and most decidedly 'unfeminine.' Ultimately, they must be destroyed or contained if order—i.e., male-dominated order—is to be restored" (Kales, 2003, p. 1632). I want to suggest that the figure of the stalking bride in contemporary African American film as witnessed in *Head of State* and *The Brothers* draws on formulas from this mainstream Hollywood genre. Indeed, the woman's wielding of the gun—a classic phallic symbol—can be interpreted as a manifestation of the castration anxieties that attend this complex genre as described by Kales.

The opening sequence with Jackson and his therapist anticipates the film's strong investments in the male psyche from a psychological or psychoanalytic perspective. These investments are subtly apparent in his mother's apparent allusion to Freud, in his sister's academic interest in studying psychology, in Sheila's sexual inhibitions that reflect "psychological barriers" that have come from indoctrination by her mother, in the senility of

Derek's mother, in the linking of Brian's obsession with White women to his mother's failure to demonstrate affection to him and his brother, and in Jackson's mother's identification of a man's willingness to give his last piece of food to a woman as an "unconscious" illustration of love and the best test of it. They are boldly manifest in the Freudian Oedipal narrative from Greek mythology in which Oedipus, the King of Thebes, unknowingly kills his father and marries his mother (who hangs herself when learning the truth), in suggesting that there is a (sexual) power struggle between father and son. It drives the main plot, including Jackson's discovery that Denise once dated his father, just when he is overcoming his fears of commitment. Once the truth comes out, Jackson accuses Denise of attempting to use "reverse psychology" on him. The struggles in the film are not only between father and son or Black men and Black women, but also between generations, and the past issues must be resolved, as symbolized in the reunion and literal remarriage ceremony of Jackson's parents, before the younger characters can claim a future.

The film attempts to debunk a range of stereotypes of Black womanhood through Brian, a lawyer who refers to a Black woman judge he once dated as an "evil bitter Black whore" and swears off dating Black women because they come with "too much drama, fake hair, excess weight, government cheese, and too many babies." Brian's scathing attacks on Black women are repeatedly interrogated and discredited by Jackson, Derek, and especially Terry, who has to be held back from attacking him physically on several occasions because of his cruelty toward "sisters." The theme of authenticity and "keeping it real" underpins constructions of gender and race. It surfaces in this film when Brian encourages his friends to recognize and admit that "We're single Black professional men. We are the cream of the crop. We deserve the best. Right now, sisters ain't up to the job." That Brian is stalked by a woman throughout the film and has his car vandalized several times is implied to be a result of his attitudes, though it reinforces the predatory scripts of femininity that more generally infuse this film. What is intriguing and revealing about this character—a lawyer still grappling with the scars of coming from the "'hood" and being raised by a single, unloving mother—is that class is so prominent in his sense of Black masculine selfhood and view of Black women. The film illustrates the complexity of his struggle to claim and inhabit a middle-class identity, a conflict evident in his continued occupation of the crime-ridden neighborhood that becomes the backdrop for the confrontation in Bebe's struggle with Terry. Indeed, the images of cars, expensive suits, luxurious apartments, and lucrative careers all underscore the relevance of class in defining all four of the main male characters.

Interestingly, in *The Brothers*, the escapist narrative centered on the Black male middle-class embracing of less ambitious Black women is not as evident as in *Head of State*, perhaps because the alternative is White women.

Brian views White women as being willing to serve him, as cheerfully saying "Okay!" to whimsical requests, as less confrontational and, again, as knowing their place. The stereotypes of race, sexuality, and gender that are at the heart of the scripts of Black women as ideal love objects are implicit elsewhere in this genre of film. Brian deserts his new White girlfriend when she fails to live up to his expectations and in public, hits the judge he once dated for insulting her, which compromises his efforts to maintain respectability as a lawyer. In the end, Brian's challenge is to resolve the tensions with his mother as a man who grew up impoverished and felt that he had not been shown enough love by her. His anger is projected onto Black women, who embody his mother, and tacitly shapes his rationale for dating White women. Instead of emphasizing differences between Black upper- and lower-class women, the film emphasizes differences between Black and White women, and ultimately implies such differences to be imagined and superficial.

While Terry and Bebe resolve their differences and Jackson overcomes his fears and finds love with Denise, questions should nevertheless be raised about what is at stake in the image of the stalking bride, scripting stereotypes of Black women as combative, predatory, angry, and potentially violent. At the most extreme, such images reflect an arrogant, presumptuous, misogynistic fantasy that every Black woman is desperate and out to *get* a Black man like "the brothers" who are, as Brian puts it, "the cream of the crop." This image of the stalking Black "bride" firing at Black men recasts and in effect feminizes perpetrators of violence in Black male life. In other words, in this film, the stalking bride has symbolically replaced the gangs the "brothers" have escaped by climbing the social ladder, as Morris Chestnut from *Boyz n the Hood* exemplifies.

The Brothers self-consciously critiques and attempts to provide a male-centered counternarrative to the widely popular 1995 femme fest film *Waiting to Exhale* based on the 1992 novel by Terry McMillan that foregrounded the experiences of four female friends. Even if it is flawed to the extent that it compromises its ostensible critique of Black female stereotypes, *The Brothers* is also visionary in highlighting four men who are committed to one another as friends and invested in an ongoing dialogue on matters of spirituality, sexuality, and mental health. This dimension not only illustrates what is perhaps a growing cultural interest among Black men to build communion among themselves in ways that parallel the support groups, book clubs, and other resources women have access to but it also suggests that male-centered activities such as basketball games provide outlets for dialogue that are effective, meaningful, and sustaining in the lives of men. Most significantly, this film attempts to displace the pervasive images of Black men as "tough" by illustrating, in the words of the author Audrey B. Chapman, that "Black men do feel about love" and do not view it as something beyond their masculine self-definition (Chapman, 1993, pp. 213–26).

THE BETTER WOMAN IN *THE BEST MAN*

Written and directed by Malcolm Lee, *The Best Man* heralded the genre of African American marriage movies and has been one of the most popular to date. Like *The Brothers*, *The Best Man* highlights the friendship and love relationships of four young Black male professionals, Harper, Quentin, Murch, and Lance. Lance has just received a lucrative contract to play pro football and is engaged to marry longtime love Mia. Harper, Lance's best man, struggles with his fears regarding love and commitment, along with his anxiety about how his friends will react to his forthcoming novel based on their relationships. In the days before the wedding, the action centers on Lance's reading of the novel and discovery that Harper and Lance's fiancée Mia once slept together. The predictable outrage that follows is a fraternal twist on the classic father-son Oedipal narrative in *The Brothers*. Harper also reconnects with a former girlfriend, Jordan Armstrong.

Jordan, now highly successful in her media career and the opposite of Harper's present caterer girlfriend Robin, is the ideal woman in his mind and the basis of the character Kendall in his novel, while Lance feels that Jordan is "too sassy and independent" and that "a woman like that don't need no man; she's one step from a lesbian." By the end of the film, Harper has realized that though Robin lacks Jordan's drive and ambition and does not have the best taste in clothing, Robin is the right woman for him, and proposes marriage to her at Mia and Lance's reception. This is clearly the right and responsible choice in the film, especially in light of how supportive Robin has been.

Jordan is the only character who fails to find a satisfying relationship. This sends the message that successful women end up alone and grimly reinforces marital statistics that reveal that the higher up the economic and educational ladder Black women climb, the less likely they are to marry. While the class contrast between Jordan and Robin is revealing, it is even more ostensible in the interplay between Murch and Shelby, another couple in the group of friends. Shelby, an upper-middle-class woman who shops at elite stores comes across as a controlling, emasculating, elitist, self-pitying, whining woman who pressures Murch to take a job at a prestigious law firm and to stop "babysitting ghetto children." Shelby is the basis for the most unflattering and loathsome character in Harper's book. Moreover, she tries to discourage Murch from attending what she describes as a "juvenile bachelor party" with his friends, where she suspects that he will talk to "hoochie mamas," a contemporary urban slang term for women who dress scantily and gaudily to attract male attention. These fears are realized in his encounter at the party with Candy, a stripper he first feels uncomfortable with, until she does a lap dance for him at the behest of his friends. As Murch attempts to get her contact information at the car, he is impressed that she knows the work of poet Audre Lorde. He breaks up with Shelby the very next day with the following words of explanation: "I am not the man for you and you are not the woman for me." He then attends the ceremony with Candy.

Like *Head of State* and *The Brothers*, *The Best Man* ostensibly draws on the logic of realness and authenticity in constructing gender and race. In a dialogue among the men during a card game, Lance underscores that in the real world (i.e., as a grown-up), he has embraced marriage as sacred and suggests that it is a cure for promiscuity. He identifies Mia as his "earth," and as a woman whose primary roles will be that of wife and mother rather than a career, suggesting her as the best counterpoint to women like Shelby and Jordan. *The Best Man* presents a masculinist narrative that maligns upwardly mobile Black middle-class women in the sense of validating highly conventional scripts of Black womanhood.

The immensely popular *Soul Food* presents similar images of Black middle-class women. In this instance, a Black woman lawyer is depicted as being so incapable of satisfying and relating to her husband that he pursues an affair with her reprobate younger cousin. To add to this, her younger sister, who stole her boyfriend when they were teenagers and eventually married him, is curiously described by the family matriarch as the "strongest" of the three sister siblings, even though in terms of careers she has not been as successful. The scenes embedded in *The Best Man* that involve Murch, Shelby and Candy are also in keeping, of course, with the classic filmic "Cinderella stories" in which a woman finds her prince and enters a more privileged realm of economic and social opportunity, a theme that has been most saliently evident in the 1991 film *Pretty Woman*, in which the prostitute portrayed by Julia Roberts is commissioned to serve as an escort for a few days by a wealthy business executive and ultimately wins his love.

Why have so many contemporary African American films been vested in presenting satirical and condemnatory models of Black middle-class women? What is at stake in these narratives related to "crisis" in Black male life? In recent years, contestations have been pervasive against women who wish to "have it all:" a career, marriage, and motherhood. This is a dialogue that Veronica Chambers explores revealingly in relation to Black women in her book *Having It All: Black Women and Success* (Chambers, 2003). More recently, Riché Daniel Barnes has discussed upper-class Black women, marriage and mothering in her anthropological study *Raising the Race: Black Career Women Redefine Marriage, Motherhood, and Community* (Barnes, 2016). Conversely, rhetorical monikers such as "the stay at home mom" and "the soccer mom," are heavily raced and classed. This comes as no surprise in a political climate dominated by political conservatives. In the same way, these films recast the masculinist ideology on family values and its seeming idealization of the domestic sphere as the ideal place of women.

Given persistent representations of Black women as pathological in the political and public spheres, the filmic scripts of Black femininity as deviant and predatory not only conform to formulas of popular cinema that portray preying, psychotic women, but in a larger political sense, they also reinforce neoconservative ideologies of Black womanhood in relation to the middle class as a complement to the "welfare queens" of the working class. Such ideologies were patently evident in the portrayal of law professor Anita Hill, whose charges of sexual harassment led to the Senate Judiciary Committee's investigation of Clarence Thomas in 1991 prior to his confirmation to the Supreme Court. As Wahneema Lubiano reveals in her essay on the Thomas hearings, terms such as "Black lady" and "welfare queen" seem contradictory but share common ground in being "recognized by the national public as stories that describe the world in particular and politically loaded ways, which is why they are constructed, reconstructed, manipulated, and contested" (Lubiano, 1992, pp. 323–363). The "Black lady," the stereotype of the overachieving Black woman that Lubiano describes, is resonant in filmic caricatures of Black middle-class women.

It is important to recognize, too, that these implied narratives of the Black middle-class woman as detrimental to Black male success and happiness reflect a larger historical economy of raced and gendered stereotypes. It is widely known, for instance, that in a nation invested in White supremacy and Jim Crow, Black women were frequently accepted as domestics, even as Black men were considered to be undesirable and unacceptable employees. This disparity in the work opportunities for Black men and women placed Black women in the position of being the major earner and radically contradicted the dominant patriarchal social order. Daniel Patrick Moynihan's 1965 *Report on the Negro Family*, which suggested that Black families were fundamentally "matriarchal" and led by castrating women, also inflected ideologies that first gained widespread momentum and acceptance during the Black liberation movement of the 1960s. It also feeds impressions that Black women are more privileged than Black men, and that they are not allies in the struggle against racism and White patriarchy.

In this larger context, it is useful to consider the misogynistic narratives of middle class, upwardly mobile Black women that animate this genre of film. It makes sense that such stereotypes would be so assertively manifest in movies about marriage, a topic which epitomizes the crisis that inflects contemporary dialogues on gender relations within the African American domestic sphere. They reflect Hollywood's long-standing stereotypes of Black women. Not much has changed in the contemporary era. Even as popular contemporary reality television shows like *The Real Housewives of Atlanta* and *Married to Medicine* highlight Black marital relationships, middle- and upper-middle-class Black women on the shows are portrayed as being combative and are frequently linked to the historical "controlling images" analyzed by Patricia Hill Collins (1990) in *Black Feminist Thought: Knowledge, Consciousness and the Politics of Empowerment.*

As public dialogues, these films, which register anxieties about the social disparities between black women and black men in the contemporary era, do not address the issues with sufficient complexity and clarity. The March 30, 2003, cover of *Newsweek* magazine announced that *"From Schools to Jobs, Black Women Are Rising Much Faster Than Black Men. What It Means for Work, Family, and Race Relations."* This *Newsweek* cover features images of Beyoncé Knowles, Star Jones, and Mellody Hobson, and is complemented by Ellis Cose's story entitled "The Black Gender Gap." To explain the existing disparities among Black women and men in the contemporary era, Veronica Chambers has argued that a "revolution" of sorts has occurred among women, who were impacted by both the civil rights movements and the women's movement (Chambers, 2003, p. 17). This is no doubt true to an extent, but what such conversations about the increasing disparity between Black men and Black women belie is Black women's expendability within the educational and labor systems in the contemporary era, as well as their growing rates of incarceration. As Black feminists, including prominent critics such as law professor Kimberlé Williams Crenshaw, have noted, President Obama's inauguration of the policy initiative My Brother's Keeper in 2014, which is designed to promote mentoring of boys of color by male leaders, is premised on logic that obscures systemic issues that impact Black girls and other girls of color.

CONCLUSION

In mainstream cinema, the shift toward examining White masculinity in relation to family and fathering that began in the late 1980s reflected the more nuanced views of masculinity advocated within studies of masculinity and gender that had mainly centered on White men. It was evident by the late 1990s in filmic representations of Black men who were grappling with relationships and marriage or with their roles as husbands and fathers. In these African American films, the shift toward an emphasis on issues such as commitment, marriage, friendship, and love in the lives of Black men in effect moved Black popular culture toward a more wide-ranging representation of Black male identity and toward a closer look at Black love relationships. In focusing mainly on Black men in the middle class, the films that I have examined demonstrate the complicated process of Black masculine fashioning even in the lives of Black men with economic privilege. Indeed, when many of the other social obstacles that Black men have conventionally faced are absent, problems concerning marriage and relationships have the potential to become all the more apparent.

Orlando Patterson has illustrated that negotiating marriage and love relationships is often just as difficult or even more difficult for Black men who are middle class than they are for Black men who are poor (Patterson, 1998). It will be increasingly important to produce a more complex analysis on class as far as Black masculinity is concerned and to acknowledge that class can be a highly unruly and unstable category in the African American context, as a character like Brian in *The Brothers* illustrates. To be sure, we need to recognize that Black middle-class men often face struggles in the social context that are very similar to those of poorer Black men, and that upward mobility does not *always* guarantee education or immunity from the abuses of law enforcement and the criminal justice system.

The theme of male friendships, and particularly the theme of forgiveness in *The Brothers* and *The Best Man*, makes the comparison relevant. However, one limitation is that even as these films aim to highlight Black male friendships and to address Black male interiority, they focus inordinately on women, making them the prioritized and almost exclusive point of reference for Black masculine formation. What these films say about femininity is therefore key to understanding the complex discourse on masculinity. Ultimately, the reactionary representations of Black women reproduce the kinds of stereotypes that undermine African American gender relations, that prohibit a more enabling dialogue on gender relations in the African American context, and that reinforce the continuing problems in African American representation that have characterized Hollywood films. Indeed, these films derail and undermine their most promising critical trajectories as they insistently recuperate Hollywood's problematic "backlash" formulas. In registering anxieties that many African Americans, and especially men, have wrestled with regarding marriage and relationships, these films suggest the urgency of a more sustained and complex critical dialogue about marriage and relationships in the African American context.

At the same time, I want to be clear that my intent here has by no means been to idealize or reify marriage as a relational model in the Black community, in the process of discussing the relationships represented across these films. It is rather, to throw into relief ways in which their narrative logic presents grossly stereotypical images of Black women, and reinforces reactionary raced, sexed, and gendered scripts of blackness that have been routinely exploited and propagated within the neoconservative political arena. Moreover, they frame marriage as the primary mechanism through which upwardly mobile Black men might achieve social and psychic peace and stability while paradoxically sanctioning stereotypes of successful, high-achieving Black women. Perhaps the *best* lesson that we can learn from these films, is that to envision and obtain more enabling forms of Black love, it is necessary to look and think beyond the conventional stereotypes and images of blackness, and in the words of Langston Hughes, be free within ourselves.

REFERENCES

Barnes, R. D. (2016). *Raising the Race: Black Career Women Redefine Marriage, Motherhood, and Community.* New York: Rutgers.
Chapman, A. B. (1993). "Black Men Do Feel about Love." In *Wild Women Don't Wear No Blues: Black Women Writers on Love, Men, and Sex,* ed. Marita Golden. New York: Doubleday, 213–26.
Chambers, V. (2003). *Having It All: Black Women and Success.* New York: Doubleday.
Cheng, A. (2001). *The Melancholy of Race: Psychoanalysis, Assimilation, and Hidden Grief.* New York: Oxford University Press.
Collins, P. H. (1990). *Black Feminist Thought: Knowledge, Consciousness and the Politics of Empowerment.* New York: Routledge.
DuBois, W. E. B. (1903). *The Souls of Black Folk,* ed. H. L. Gates, Jr. (2014). New York, Oxford University Press.
DuCille, A. (1993). *The Coupling Convention: Sex, Text and Tradition in Black Women's Fiction.* New York: Oxford University Press.
Freeman, E. (2002). *The Wedding Complex: Forms of Belonging in Modern American Culture.* Durham: Duke University Press.
Kales, E. F. (2003). "Body Double as Body Politic: Psychosocial Myth and Cultural Binary in Fatal Attraction." *The International Journal of Psychoanalsyis, 84*(6): 1631–37.
Lane, C. ed. (1998). *The Psychoanalysis of Race.* New York: Columbia University Press.
Lubiano, W. (1992). "Black Ladies, Welfare Queens and State Minstrels: Ideological War by Narrative Means." In *Race-ing Justice, En-gendering Power: Essays on Anita Hill, Clarence Thomas, and the Construction of Social Reality,* ed. T. Morrison. New York: Pantheon Books, 323–63.
Madhubuti, H. (1989). *Black Men: Obsolete, Single, Dangerous?* Chicago: Third World Press.
Moynihan, D. P. (1965). *The Negro Family: The Case for National Action,* Washington, D.C.: Office of Policy Planning and Research, U.S. Department of Labor.
Nelson, D. D. (1998). *National Manhood: Capitalist Citizenship and the Imagined Fraternity of White Men.* Durham: Duke University Press.
Patterson, O. (1998). *Rituals of Blood: Consequences of Slavery in Two American Centuries.* New York: Basic Books, 163.
Spillers, H. (2003). *Black, White and in Color.* Chicago: University of Chicago Press.
Tate, C. (1998). *Psychoanalysis and Black Novels.* New York: Oxford University Press.

Chapter Seven

The Aftermath of *Act Like a Lady, Think Like a Man*

The Real Dilemma for African American Women in Finding the Love They Want

Dale Williams

The first time I tried to read *Act Like a Lady, Think Like a Man* by Steve Harvey and Denene Millner, I could not make it to the second half of the book. More than ten years later, while exploring the decline of Black marriages and failed relationships, the book emerged in my research. It became very clear that women, especially African American women favored the message and saw it as valuable advice. Yet, I had serious issues with the book, which I kept to myself because I knew how others viewed the message. I, like others, favored Harvey's work as an entertainer. Appearing to disagree with the core theme of the book, to me, would be betrayal. I did not want to seem as if I, a Black woman, was not supporting, Harvey, a Black man. I also did not want to face the fact that this book and other statistics in this research directly dealt with me as a single Black female. More importantly, I feared the backlash that I knew accosted some African American female writers who have openly criticized their male counterparts on such issues. I did not desire the label of a feminist, nor the tagline of an angry Black female. Yet I was angry and disappointed. Consequently, like many women in 2009, I bought the book, but unlike many, I found no value in it. It only proved what I knew all along: in order for women to be successful in long-term relationships, they had to do the bulk of the work.

The African American female is in a precarious position, and it is one that she cannot always speak freely about as sometimes there are no words to describe the awkward space in which she finds herself. She does not fit comfortably in the fabric of the American dream, which promises that if you work hard, you can have anything you want. Furthermore, everything about the African American female contradicts the American idea of womanhood. Yet the African American woman has worked hard, excelled, and in many cases become the best and the brightest. But among all of her accomplishments she appears to fail at obtaining a lasting relationship. Thus, Harvey's message spoke directly to an apparent deficiency and a real need in African American females to obtaining the one thing in which she could not seem to accomplish—a good man. Unfortunately, Harvey's book for many women did not turn out to be the perfect playbook, as advertised; rather it was really a "how to book" for pleasing your man.

In exploring the basis of his message, Harvey (2009) said, that he began to impart advice to women based on one concept, that he lives by, which is "how to be a man." He added that he spent countless hours talking to friends, all of whom are men. According to Harvey (2009), all men basically think in similar ways. In addition, Harvey (2009) explained that he teaches women to have a clear-eyed knowing approach to dealing with men on their terms, turf, and way so that women can get exactly what they want. Yet this theory is problematic because women are still not getting what they want; and Harvey's recommendations for women to transform themselves so that they can have successful relationships suggests that women cannot be who they are authentically and get what they want out of a relationship. Lang (2012) countered by saying, "The message here is that women can be strong and empowered, only as long as their power or success still caters to male power and ego" (para. 2). Thus, when Harvey says that all men are simple, and women must think like them, this is contradictory and bizarre. Although the book was written for women, Harvey (2009) admitted that initially he toyed with the idea of writing a book in response to his listeners from his radio show that would help men and women. However, Harvey deliberately focused his entire book on women, although he has no authority as a female to speak from this point of view. This may not be an issue, but when Harvey says that he has the authority from "being a man" to tell women how to get a man, he takes on a masculine point of view, which puts women at a deficiency. Harvey says men are simple which implies that the woman is then not smart enough nor does she know enough to maintain a relationship with a man.

The man in Harvey's book is an oxymoron because he is more than simple but also the unobtainable prize. Even more disturbing, Harvey tries to side with his female audience by referencing his daughters, saying that one day, "They will all grow up and reach for the same dream most women have: The husband. Some kids. A house. A happy life. True love" (p. 5). Yet these comments are nothing more than "old school sexism" while some women want such things, not all are dreaming about it. Some women are dreaming of a successful career among other things, thus Harvey's remarks are steeped in traditional masculinity. Harvey, like a savior figure, says women need "a voice, someone to help get them through and decipher the muck, so they can get what they're truly after" (p. 5). Thus, he promised in his book to reveal the secrets of men so that women can live happily ever after, believing that after these secrets are uncovered they will understand the man better and have a fulfilling relationship. How desperate are we for relationship advice that this book, which ignores the totality of being an African American woman, serves as a self-help guide to finding a man by thinking like one?

DOMINATE BY NATURE

It can be argued that the African American woman is dominant by nature; furthermore, her African roots suggest she is matriarchal although some critics combat this research. Fortunately, this does not negate her experiences, which always antagonize traditional gender roles in American culture. Contrary to Harvey's message, rarely does the African American woman have the time to "Act like a Lady" and seldom is she not "Thinking like a Man." The truth of the matter is that her thinking like a man is what has contributed to her singleness. The African American woman is often the foundation of her family; if she is not the head of her household, she usually runs it. Many African American women, who have significant others, still complain of taking on the bulk of the responsibility in the household; therefore, seemingly doing it alone. Moynihan (1965) wrote that Black women were violating traditional gender roles by being too strong and independent. He suggested that Black men should participate in the military in order to masculinize themselves. These comments, of course, infuriated the African American male community at the time. Over the years, many scholars disputed and dismissed this matriarch thesis as an insult to African American men. Yet what Moynihan's (1965) research explained was that slavery had initiated a single-mother structure that excluded meaningful participation by Black men thus rendering them incapable to conform to traditional norms of masculinity. The report was crucified, but the reality of the research still lingers as African American women are even more dominant emotionally, personally, and professionally.

Most African American women admit to being raised by their mothers to dominate. As a result, the African American woman has been prepared to live independently, if necessary, unlike her male counterpart, who has often been cuddled by African American mothers, hence the necessity of the section in Harvey's book entitled "Mama's Boys." African American women who experience this type of upbringing are taught to be independent and oftentimes their dominance cannot be contained or suppressed. Consequently, they are often misunderstood and mistreated because of it. Wallace (2007) described this dilemma this way:

> Let's face it, Black women have, for centuries, been taught how to be "fathers"—protectors and providers for their families—in fact, they have been expected to know how. Black men, however, have not been taught how to be "mothers"—how to nurture partners, family and friends in emotional ways; how to put their own wants and desires aside for the benefit of the group and how to find joy and fulfillment in that which they create and care for. (p. 19)

Perhaps there are times when African American women want to take on a more passive role and "Act like a Lady," but she does not have time for such frivolity. Therefore, she is not at home trying to figure out how to please her man or even how to get one because she has children to raise, bills to pay, and work to do. And yes, she is aware that amid her doing it all, there is a chance she may be doing it alone. Thus, she has learned how to accept and navigate this space. Sadly, the reality of the situation as Banks (2012) pointed out is "Nearly seven out of every ten black women are unmarried and as many as three out of ten may never marry. For black women, being unmarried has become the new normal, single the new black" (p. 6).

THE NUMBERS IMBALANCE

Harvey failed to address the lack of opportunities that African American women have in comparison to African American men in finding a mate in his book. Yet he does identify that woman are losing the game of a winning relationship due to their lack of understanding of what drives and motivates men (Harvey and Millner, 2009). Harvey's failure to acknowledge the numbers imbalance is misleading to African American women, who often place the blame of not having a man on themselves. The numbers imbalance is one of the consistent problems attributed to the decline in African American relationships and marriages. Simply put, there is a lack of availability of Black males due to mass incarceration, interracial marriages, and economic status. In addition, Black women are the least likely than any other ethnic group to marry outside of her race, further limiting her choices. Here is where we find the Black woman, alone amid staggering statistics that confirm she is not only the least likely of any other race to marry but has the least amount of options to do so. Meanwhile her partner, the "simple" Black man, rides off into the sunset with unlimited possibilities. Banks (2012) reported:

> With African Americans, in contrast, the numbers imbalance favors men. What this means is that for a black man and black woman negotiating a relationship, the man will have more options and more opportunities outside the relationship than the woman. If for whatever reason their relationship

negotiation breaks down—if they can't agree about what sort of relationship to have—the man will encounter surfeit of beautiful, accomplished, single black women. The woman, in contrast, will have to contend with a much shallower pool of desirable men. (p. 61)

Jackson (1971) who wrote "But Where Are the Men" reminds us that there has been a continuous decline in the number of Black males available to Black females since 1850. Banks (2012) identified some major reasons for this imbalance:

First, black men's incarceration constricts the market for poor and working-class black women. Second, interracial marriage depletes the pool of men for middle-class, college-educated black women. Third, the economic prospects for many men have worsened while those for women have improved. (p. 29)

Therefore, Harvey knowing that Black women do not have an adequate pool of men to choose from turns his message of empowerment into a call for submissiveness. Therefore, despite his overall success in giving African American women advice on relationships, he has left them no better than he found them. Due to the numbers imbalance, most African American women cannot find compatible men with whom to have a relationship and many settle in order to have or maintain one. A study by Vaterlaus, Skogrand, and Chaney (2015) focused on positive marital qualities citing that being equally yoked was a major factor for success in marriage. Therefore, if men and women are not compatible or in an equally yoked situation from the onset, the relationship usually does not last. Consequently, many women spend a lot of time trying to turn the man into something they want him to be and morphing themselves into something they are not. While Harvey's book focuses on capturing the man of her dreams, his message does little to help the woman who cannot find a man. More importantly, his one-sided advice ignores the fundamental needs of the African American woman who also wants her desires met. There is more to just having the man of your dreams, women also want him to be able to cater to her as well. Harvey and Millner (2009) insinuate that women must compromise themselves, by altering their behavior to fulfill their dreams. African American women find themselves limited, ignored, and smothered emotionally by such advice.

So why are Black women buying this message? Black women are buying messages like Harvey's because of constant statistical data like Banks, which reports that Black women are on the bottom of the marriage pool. "Some of these women live with the creeping sense that they may never marry" (Banks, 2012). "As a result of the black male shortage, there is an intense competition for the available few" (Aborampah, 1989). Thus, as one critic asserts the female may have to bargain on the male's own terms (Aborampah, 1989). Therefore, Harvey's book is nothing more than a bargaining tool that ultimately diminishes a woman's character and self-esteem. He directly speaks to the fear that Black women have about marriage and gives them a sense of proactive steps to try and change the odds against them. Hence, his book is entertaining but ineffective. Despite Harvey's compromising advice, for some African American women the book at the time seemed like the only answer to an ongoing problem in Black love.

BLACK LOVE

When Harvey's book, *Act Like a Lady, Think Like a Man*, was published in 2009, it seemed to awaken the topic of Black love. In some ways, it gave women a glimmer of hope, in that finally African American men had spoken and acknowledged things from a female perspective. Harvey even dedicated the book to all women, with hope that it would "empower" them to have a deeper look into the minds of men. Surprisingly, the book spent two years on the *New York Times* hardcover for advice best-seller's list, and was number one for twenty-three weeks. In addition, the popularity of the book led to a top grossing movie (*Think Like a Man*) followed by another book sequel called *Straight Talk, No Chaser*, which had equal success. Harvey's book seemed to have reawakened the conversations and concerns about Black love and his Hollywood success at the box office proved people were interested. The backlash of the publication of the book did not just spark success for Harvey but similar themes in film, television, and talk and reality shows followed.

In 2017, the OWN network debuted the docu-series "Black Love" with 1.2 million total viewers. According to the network (2017), the series became OWN's most-watched unscripted series to debut in their history and the network's highest-rated unscripted series, proving people are desperate for answers. People were interested in Black love and the state of Black marriage. While, Harvey could be credited for revitalizing the conversation of Black love, his book however, still presented a lopsided view, which exposed the unhealthy dynamics in African American male/female relationships. According to Aborampah (1989), "Overall there seems to be general agreement about the existence of unhealthy conflicts between Black males and black females" (p. 320). The conversation of Black love—male and female relationships—has been consistent over the decades. In 1984, Clyde W. Franklin, II, tackled the topic of Black love stating that the topic is traceable as early as 1939 in Edward Franklin Frazier's book *The Negro Family in the United States*, followed by St. Clair Drake and Horace Clayton's 1945 book *Black Metropolis: A Study of Negro Life in a Northern City*. Authors Grier and Cobbs (1968), whose book *Black Rage*, in the 1960s focused on issues such as hostility of black men toward black women. The dialogue surged in the

1960s after the Black Empowerment Movement and continued to gain momentum in the 1970s.

Harvey's book proved to be timely and innovative as there is no other book written by an African American male as a self-help guide for females in relationships but his advice did not resonate enough to provoke any real change in the marriage or relationship dilemma for African Americans as numbers continued to decrease. According to Banks (2012): We are the least likely to marry and the most likely to divorce; we maintain fewer committed and enduring relationships than any other group. Not since slavery have Black men and women been as unpartnered as we are now (p. 2). Statistics prove that Black people have struggled the most in maintaining romantic relationships, partly because of outside pressures such as poor family structure, racism, and even lack of economic development. African-Americans have been systematically conditioned to prosper individually, but not as a group, consequently making them ill equipped for marriage. Such statistics give books like Harvey's a platform to give advice from a personal point of view especially when presented with a light tone. Nevertheless, the subject of Black love remains one of the most popular topics of discussion in the African American community, making people susceptible to possible explanations that may or may not be valuable thus giving entryway to messages like Harvey's. His success as a best-seller had little cultural results outside of entertainment. Harvey's success increased after his book and movie, thus leading to a daytime talk show, where his target audience is primarily female. He seems to have turned into being a relationship specialist. Meanwhile TV and film continue to capitalize on the awakening of Black love, while African Americans continue to seek ways to master it.

FEMINIST CRITICISM

Relationship books began to surge in the 1990s when people could take their minds off the economic and political issues of the '70s and '80s. As women became more independent economically, these books became a huge factor in relationships, as needs shifted from security to fulfillment. Therefore, books like Harvey's that sought fulfillment and understanding began to gain an audience but Harvey's message or suggestions were not a new theory. Dr. John Gray published a book in 1992, *Men Are from Mars, Women Are from Venus: A Practical Guide for Improving Communication and Getting What You Want in Your Relationships*. Similarly, a man was giving advice, but unlike *Think Like a Man* this book covered how men and women should conduct themselves in relationships by breaking down communication barriers. Similarly, Gray experienced instant success and had several sequels to follow. Yet such instruction was received differently and was somewhat resented when told from a female point of view. For example, in 1995, *The Rules: Time-Tested Secrets for Capturing the Heart of Mr. Right* a self-help book by authors Ellen Fein and Sherrie Schneider, gained noteworthy success but the *New York Times* best-seller's list was heavily criticized for being antifeminist for suggesting that women should not aggressively pursue men, but rather, they ought to get the men to pursue them. Anderson (2015) noted this review of the book twenty years after its publication:

Criticism of *The Rules* was primarily directed at women—that it encouraged women to play games, that it made women manipulative. But in a patriarchy, it's rational to define the needs of the powerful, to meet them, and to be chosen to share their position in the world. Historically, women haven't had a lot of agency in selecting a mate, and that history, however muted now, still influences contemporary courtship. *The Rules* proposes to correct that lack of agency by taking away even more of your agency. It could be subtitled "Strategies for Chattel" (para. 21).

This is very similar to Harvey's message, yet he has eluded such harsh feminist criticism as his book has been widely accepted and acted upon by women. Yet from a feminist standpoint, like *The Rules*, Harvey's book is also chattel, which somewhat explains why women must be coached into transforming their thinking and altering their behavior. Ironically Harvey's cowriter Denene Millner published a counter to *The Rules* in 1997, called *The Sistah Rules: Secrets for Meeting, Getting, and Keeping a Good Black Man*, the book received little success. Although Millner's *Sistah Rules* was much more liberal and seemed to challenge the rigid themes in *The Rules*, she and Harvey's book mimic characteristics of a conduct book.

Early feminist critics Gilbert and Gubar (1979) studied the concept of acting like a lady in their work and revealed that conduct books for ladies had proliferated in the eighteenth century enjoining young girls to submissiveness, modesty, selflessness, and reminding all women that they should be angelic. Gilbert and Gubar (1979) emphasized when a woman steps outside of these conforms of behavior, she is seen and described as a monster. This seems to explain accurately the negative descriptions of African American women who openly show aggression. Portrayals of African American women have been: sacrificial, strong, or self-righteous. Rarely are African American women portrayed as gentle, soft, kind, or pure. When such vulnerabilities are exposed in them, culturally it is interpreted as weakness.

Nevertheless, conduct books were not foreign to the African American community as they moved out of slavery; they began to educate themselves to assimilate as free men and women into society. As a result, such books on how to conduct oneself could also be found in schools for African American children. For example, in 1902, Dr. Charlotte Hawkins Brown founded the Alice Freeman Palmer Memorial Institute when she was nineteen years old (Brown, 2003). Over the next fifty years, it became one of the most renowned schools in the nation (Brown, 2003). Brown published an etiquette guide for young people entitled *The Correct Thing to Do, to Say, to Wear*. In her book, she referenced boy and girl relationships and courtships:

> A girl must be considerate, not overbearing or dictatorial. She must give the boy plenty of room to be gracious, chivalrous, but confident in his ability to entertain her in a wholesome manner. A girl must not do all the talking. It is the nature of man to dominate. Feed his pride by letting him get all the glory for the planning of a swell evening. (p. 75)

Such books guiding women in the appropriate behavior and the concept of "Acting like a Lady" is an old theme. Gilbert and Gubar (1979) specifically point out that part of being a lady is equated to the "arts of pleasing men." "The arts of pleasing men, in other words, are not only angelic characteristics; in more worldly terms, they are the proper acts of a lady" (Gilbert & Gubar, 1979). Likewise, Harvey's book title, *Act Like a Lady, Think Like a Man*, is in keeping with the traditional ideas in these conduct books on how to please a man and stay in a lady's place. Harvey's chosen title directly translates this primary message of pleasing men. Notably, when the book was made to the film version, the title was shortened to "Think Like a Man." One can only speculate as to why "Act Like a Lady" was appropriately dropped.

Also familiar in previous conduct guides/books are some of the personality types described in Harvey and Millner's book. Harvey reveals the dreamer who lacks responsibility; the cheater who lacks loyalty; the noncommittal who lacks commitment; and the Mama's boy who lacks accountability. However, in 1992 Terry McMillan published *Waiting to Exhale* revealing the same four male personality types. Likewise, McMillan's fiction quickly rose to fame but she was accused of male bashing. McMillan, like Harvey, also had her book adapted into a movie. Where Harvey pointed out how much a man makes defines his ability to be productive in his love relationships, McMillan pointed this out in her characterization of her male characters twenty-five years ago. Yet, men said she was not being fair to their position. However, when Harvey exposed these same male traits as major problems for women, men were silent.

In the same year, that Gilbert and Gubar published their criticism Wallace (1979) published *Black Macho and the Myth of the Superwoman* with a wave of controversy as she criticized the masculinity bias of Black politics in the '60s. Her book took on the marginalization of women by the patriarchal culture of Black Power. Like female writers before her, she took a lot of criticism from male and females from the African American community. She wrote then:

> While she stood by silently as he became a man, she assumed that he would finally glorify and dignify Black womanhood just as the White man has done for White women. Wallace goes on to say that this has not happened for Black women. (Wallace, 1979)

She paid a heavy price for such criticism. When *Black Macho and the Myth of the Superwoman* appeared in print, Wallace was twenty-six years old and unprepared for the resulting onslaught of criticism. While some members of the African American community supported her work, many others were openly hostile. Wallace was accused of causing a division in the African American community that would aid Whites; of being a dupe of White feminists who only wanted to exploit her; and of weakening the African American community. The sharp criticism gave Wallace a nervous breakdown (Wallace, 1979).

Wallace's controversial book, *Black Macho and the Myth of the Superwoman*, was rereleased thirty-seven years after its debut in 2015. Many of the things Wallace said then still resonate now and are important. The reality is African American women have been exposing the needs of African American men for a long time and giving him voice, while silencing hers. She has portrayed his strengths and his weaknesses and has never blamed him solely for the weight of the African American community's dilemmas. What Harvey demonstrates in his book by failing to acknowledge her equally continues to stagnate her journey.

THE MIND-SET OF THE BOOK

Harvey (2009) says, "If you are in a committed relationship and you are trying to get the ring—this book is for you. If you are married and you want to regain control and strengthen your bond—this book is for you." Although Harvey's book includes three major parts: The Mind-Set of a Man, Why Men Do What They Do, and The Playbook: How to Win the Game, the core mind-set of the book is having an overall understanding of men. Harvey (2009) says, "With this book you can put into play your plans, your dreams, and your desires, and best of all you can figure out if he's planning to be with you or just playing with you" (p. 7). Harvey's comments reveal the overall purpose of the book is to teach women how to understand the mind-set of a man, which will give women a better chance of maintaining the man of their dreams. This sounds more like a 1960s appliance commercial geared toward housewives.

In part 1 of the book, Harvey (2009) says that men are driven by three things: who they are, what they do, and how much money they make. Admittedly, Harvey's research for the ook was sparked from his experience as a radio host who responds to Black women who call in to talk about relationships. Although Harvey's book is not particularly based on scientifically proven research, some points align with current studies that suggest that economic fortunes drive marital outcomes. Therefore, it has been proven that the decline in marriage occurred with changes in women's labor market participation (James, 1998). Thus, in this case, Harvey's assessment is correct, men are driven by who they are, and this becomes even more challenging if he feels the woman is more accomplished than him. Another point that Harvey makes is, if the man is not particularly happy with where he is in terms of what he does, he is also incapable of being in a productive relationship. Further, if his money is limited, then he feels inadequate as a man and this becomes an issue in the relationship. Harvey (2009) admits that until the man accomplishes his goals he will be too busy to focus on a relationship. Harvey (2009) says men want to feel like they are number one and "in charge." While these are all substantial points they are also very common themes. Thus, part 1 of the book deals with primarily what drives men, how their love differentiates from women, his needs, and how he communicates. Part 2 specifies the behavior of men, and the lack of control women have in changing them, thus understanding his mind-set goes right along with accepting his behavior. Finally, part 3, guides women into how they should behave to win the game with a series of questions women always wanted to ask.

If the analogy of equating loving your partner to winning a game does not throw one off the well-meaning advice will. Despite the overall male dominated focus, rather than dismiss Harvey's ideas, it is necessary to examine his theories more closely to understand why this ideology resonated with so many women. For many women, the book gave insight to behaviors of men in which they did not understand. However, it became clear that part 1 was more about pleasing your man, more so than understanding him. Part 2 was about excusing his behavior because he will not change, and part 3 was about how to conduct one's self to gain the man of your dreams. Harvey's message is that to get the best out of your man, the woman must understand his needs, in terms of how he thinks, behaves, and reacts. It is not that women are opposed to knowing the mind-set of the man; it just shifts all of the weight of the responsibility of the relationship over to her when she already does not possess the upper hand in the situation, which puts her in a position of inferiority. As a result, she has little choice but to participate in such behavior if she wants the relationship to work or, as Harvey puts it, to win the game. Therefore, in an attempt to understand his needs, she ultimately ignores her needs. What Harvey's message revealed as the mind-set of the book is that African American men are more comfortable with traditional gender roles in which the woman's goal is to please him. However, the reality is this only works if her needs are reciprocated because the needs in a relationship cannot be at the expense of one partner.

CONCLUSION

Sociologist Orlando Patterson concluded in the late 1990s that African American women assumed leadership positions in almost all areas of the African American community and outperformed African American men at the middle- and upper-class levels socially and professionally (Banks, 2012). What Harvey understood, and why he primarily targeted African American women in his book, is that unlike her male counterpart, the African American women has accessed more opportunities and encouragers to be successful. But encased in her glorious success, the African American woman has found herself unexplainably single. In fact, in an ethnographic study in 2009, just when *Think Like a Man* was published, Rochelle Holland researched the perceptions of mate selection for marriage and the decisions of twenty-five college-educated African American mothers who chose to have children while single. The key word here is choice for many women have chosen to be single. Holland (2009) pointed out that many of the participants expressed that being in poor relationships with their child/children's father tainted their desire to marry and influenced their levels of intimacy and trust with men. One woman even reported that she did not have the necessary compromising skills required for marriage (Holland, 2009).

Harvey's book misses this point that it is not so much that women do not understand the mind-set of the man, it's just that some have chosen not to deal with it. So, Harvey is not telling women anything that they do not already know. As Black women have walked outside of the lines of role expectations, which have been an intricate part of their intimate relationships, they created conflict that African American males have never recovered from; and because men have the upper hand, African American women are expected to adjust through submission. The African American woman must choose between tragic singlehood or submissive compensation. Thus, like the women in Holland's case study, many have decided to have children on their own or be alone. As a result, Harvey's promise to lead African American women to their dream man through the mind-set of men is a ruse. Harvey narrowly focuses on turning women into what men want yet silences the voice of African American females all in the name of love. Although it may not have been profitable for Harvey to tailor his book to both a male and female audience, he could have approached the subject more diplomatically.

Finally, rather than African American women seeing themselves as the victims of the marriage crisis, our power must be invoked to look at the problem equally from both a male and female perspective. Harvey gives females a false sense of power, as she believes she controls the man, which in fact Harvey's advice has her under his (simple-man) control. However, what she must realize is the overall problem is not something which she can change alone, nor is it her sole responsibility to do so. It is not only important that she understands how her male partner thinks but he also must understand how she thinks. One without the other cancels one person out.

As previously stated, the reality is the African American woman has been championing the needs of African American men for a long time and giving him voice, while silencing her own. She has shouldered his strengths and his weaknesses; and has never blamed him solely for the weight of the African American community's dilemmas. Our work must continue as both African American males and females move away from old arguments and look beyond outside pressures for the decline, success, or even the breakdown of African American marriages and relationships. What we learned from Harvey ten years ago is that not much has changed. While Harvey's book is credited for reintroducing the topic of conversation regarding Black love and even fueling some excitement, his sexist approach does more harm than good to an already controversial topic. At times, his suggestions are more like ultimatums rather than friendly advice. He missed the internal conflict that both the Black man and the Black woman must contend with due to equally produced poor communication, unrealistic expectations, and lack of preparedness to work collectively. Harvey (2009) says there are women who can run a small business, keep a household with three kids in tiptop shape, and chair a church group all at the same time, but cannot figure out what makes men tick. Dear Mr. Harvey, the African American woman understands the African American man just fine, she is just tired of running backward. Also, Mr. Harvey, since you conclude that the way I, a strong, Black, and phenomenal woman can help the African American man get there—a happy, healthy, and committed relationship—is to help him focus on his dream, see the vision, and implement his plan, I wonder, while I am helping him get there, who is helping ME?

Zora Neale Hurston's words are louder than ever, "The nigga woman is the mule of the world."

REFERENCES

Aborampah, O. (1989). "Black Male-Female Relationships: Some Observations." *Journal of Black Studies, 19*(3), 320–42. Retrieved from http://www.jstor.org/stable/2784662

Anderson, L. (2015, April 8). "*The Rules*, 20 Years Later: Why Do Men and Women Still Follow the Same Old Dating Script?" Vox. Retrieved from http://www.vox.com/2015/4/8/8353915/rules-dating-advice.

Banks, R. R. (2012). *Is Marriage for White People?: How the African American Marriage Decline Affects Everyone.* New York: Plume.

Brown, C. H. (2003). *The Correct Thing to Do, to Say, to Wear.* Boston, MA: Christopher Pub. House.

Fein, E., & Schneider, S. (1995). *The Rules: Time-Tested Secrets for Capturing the Heart of Mr. Right.* New York: Warner Books.

Franklin, C. W. (1984). "Black Male-Black Female Conflict: Individually Caused and Culturally Nurtured." *Journal of Black Studies, 15*(2), 139–54. https://doi.org/10.1177/002193478401500201

Gilbert, S. M., & Gubar, S. (1979). *The Madwoman in the Attic: The Woman Writer and the Nineteenth-Century Literary Imagination.* Yale University Press.

Gray, J. (1992). *Men are from Mars, Women are from Venus: A Practical Guide for Improving Communication and Getting What You Want in Your Relationships.* New York: HarperCollins.

Grier, W. H., & Cobbs, P. M. (1968). *Black Rage.* New York: Basic Books.

Harvey, S., & Millner, D. (2009). *Act Like a Lady, Think Like a Man: What Men Really Think about Love, Relationships, Intimacy, and Commitment.* New York: Amistad.

Holland, R. (2009). "Perceptions of Mate Selection for Marriage among African American, College-Educated, Single Mothers." *Journal of Counseling & Development, 87*(2), 170–78. doi:10.1002/j.1556-6678.2009.tb00564.x

Jackson, J. (1971). "But Where Are the Men?" *The Black Scholar, 3*(4), 30–41. Retrieved from http://www.jstor.org/stable/41203707

James, A. D. (1998). "What's Love Got to Do with It?: Economic Viability and the Likelihood of Marriage among African American Men." *Journal of Comparative Family Studies, 29*(2), 373–86. Retrieved from https://bethelu.idm.oclc.org/login?url=https://search.ebscohost.com/login.aspx?direct=true&db=a9h&AN=1464823&site=ehost-live

Lang, N. (2012, June 26). "Think Like a Man Isn't Just Sexist: It's Offensive to Pretty Much Everyone." Retrieved from https://www.huffingtonpost.com/nico-lang/think-like-a-man-is-offensive_b_1449409.html.

McMillan, T. (1992). *Waiting to Exhale.* New York: Viking.

Millner, D. (1997). *The Sistahs' Rules: Secrets for Meeting, Getting, and Keeping a Good Black Man Not to be Confused with the Rules.* New York: William Morrow and Company.

Moynihan, D. P. (1965). "The Negro Family: The Case for National Action." Washington, DC: U.S. Department of Labor, Office of Planning and Research.

Vaterlaus, J., Skogrand, L., and Chaney, C. (2015). "Help-Seeking for Marital Problems: Perceptions of Individuals in Strong African American Marriages." *Contemporary Family Therapy: An International Journal, 37*(1): 22–32. doi:10.1007/s10591-014-9324-4.

Wallace, D. M. (2007). "It's a M-A-N Thang": Black Male Gender Role Socialization and the Performance of Masculinity in Love Relationships." *Journal of Pan African Studies, 1*(7), 11+. Retrieved from http://link.galegroup.com.bethelu.idm.oclc.org/apps/doc/A192394156/AONE?u=tel_a_bethelc&sid=AONE&xid=da5a6ec3.

Wallace, M. (2015). *Black Macho and the Myth of the Superwoman.* New York: Verso.

Chapter Eight

Mental Health and Interpersonal Relationships

A Personal Essay

Karen McMeo

"It's not you, it's me." When an ex-boyfriend said these words to me, I immediately thought that it was his way of saying that something was wrong with me. However, after I started seeing a therapist, I realized that it was him, *and* me. During the first three months following the unexpected breakup, my best friend, who lives in another state, was my daily audience of one as I cried and dissected the relationship. Eventually, I saw the signs that I had missed and the warning bells that I ignored. However, there continued to be a disconnect between my head and heart. It was that disconnect that made me continue "dating him" after the breakup, accepting his sporadic calls, visits, and impromptu dates. Despite the declarations that Will made during his breakup speech of how selfish he was, that work was his mistress, and that he wouldn't be a good husband, my heart was stubborn. It felt sorry for the obviously deeply wounded man who needed help and time. Ironically, during one of his visits a few months later, he told me that I shouldn't think that giving him a certain amount time would make a difference.

On the advice of my male friend, I stopped initiating calls to Will. I didn't think that I could go through with it, and each day was an internal battle. But, not calling turned out to be a major turning point for me. After two weeks, he left a voicemail message to see how my daughter and I were doing. I didn't return his call until the next day or two. Eventually, after a few more conversations, our communications ceased.

After months of my best friend giving me both gentle and tough love, I finally started to hear her and see what I couldn't and didn't previously want to see. Then I started to berate myself for being so naive and trusting. She pointed out that I wasn't strong enough to accept the truth and that I kept hoping for the best without preparing for the worst. It had become apparent that I was going through the five stages of grief—denial, anger, bargaining, depression, and acceptance (Kübler-Ross and Kessler, 2005). Naturally, the stages didn't always come neatly—one at a time and in order—but, in random order or in pairs, and always on repeat. During the acceptance stage, my mind knew that Will and I were ill-matched and wouldn't survive a marriage, unless I further comprised myself by shelving the needs, wants, and desires that I had for living my best life. We were incompatible spiritually, morally, and emotionally. My two confidantes said that "Will did me a favor" and that I had "dodged a bullet." Despite all of my head knowledge, my heart still refused to give up and continued mourning for the "potential man" that I loved and the future that I had imagined. I continued to contemplate why I wasn't worth an effort from him to overcome his issues and make us work. Finally, my best friend said that my refusal to let the relationship die and let go of the corpse suggested that I had deeper issues. I had to agree. My grief over a mere mortal man was excessive and alarming. So, I followed her suggestion to see a professional.

After weeks of the therapist listening to me recount my entire time with Will and trying to figure out how this happened to me, what signs did I miss, and how would I survive the breakup, she pondered out loud if my relationship with Will had something to do with my parents. I was confused and stunned. She intimated that being with Will was familiar, as he demonstrated some of the traits my parents had, such as being overly critical and emotionally unavailable. I quickly dismissed her suggestion. For a few minutes, I felt like I was a character in one of the many movies I had seen—sitting across from a therapist telling me about my mommy and daddy issues. Of course, that was possible—but it wasn't *my* story. For a moment, I tried to make the leap, but I just couldn't see it at the time.

During my grieving process, I went to the library and got a few books on relationships to help me to gain insights and help me cope. In her book, "The Breakup Bible, licensed psychotherapist Sussman (2011) introduced me to *me*. I began to examine and confront my childhood and how it shaped me. I also gained greater clarity in reading the research of Ainsworth, who in the 1960s, wrote about three attachment styles that are formed within a nuclear family—assured, ambivalent, and avoidant (as cited in Sussman, 2011, pp. 175–87). The assured style develops in the "Leave It to Beaver" and "The Cosby Show" type of families, where emotionally healthy interactions abound. The assured lifestyle was unrecognizable in my reality. However, the ambivalent and avoidant styles were very familiar. Television and movie characters with these types of personalities are Archie Bunker in "All in the Family," and Will Smith's character in *Hitch* and Don Draper in "Mad Men."

On the ambivalent side, I identified with several of the listed descriptions—having a parent who had a mood disorder, was overly critical, and unreasonably strict. In addition, my parent's disconnected marriage contributed notably. On the avoidant side, I had a parent(s) who had limited coping skills, were childlike, self-involved, emotionally void, and had parent(s) who were avoidant. It is also stated that people from avoidant families will have an increased chance of experiencing anxiety and/or depression.

The biggest breakthrough occurred instantly when I read:

> Avoidants suffer hard when love connections fall apart. They experience severe emotional and physical anguish and tend to have a greater preoccupation with their exes. Many distance themselves from others and do not seek the help they need and deserve. Others lean too hard on their support system because they do not know how to care for themselves. (p. 188)

Even though my best friend was a major support to me after my breakup, Sussman's book made me realize that I had been in an excessively co-dependent relationship with her for about three-quarters of our nearly forty-year friendship. I sought her advice on almost every aspect of my life because I did not trust my instincts to make the best decision. I was afraid to fail. The breakup and therapy sessions prompted the intense self-reflection that I needed for my journey of true self-discovery because not only did I not know who Will was, I didn't know who I was or how I came to be the person that I am.

In addition, I also realized that I was engaging in "repetition compulsion" (Sussman, 2011, p. 189). Because my parents were critical and emotionally withdrawn, I subconsciously would attract guys who had the same emotional deficit, thereby, hoping to resolve the issues with my parents vicariously through them. By attempting to please them and being overly understanding and forgiving, I expected that I would get the appreciation and approval that I couldn't get in my childhood. However, this only kept me in a hopeless loop of destruction and failure.

After my parents separated and eventually divorced when I was around eleven, my father continued to be a fixture in our life. My younger brother and I would spend weekends at his apartment and go on summer vacations with him to Canada or Disneyworld. Of course, when I became a young adult and gained some independence, phone calls replaced weekend sleepovers, and as I got older, his cantankerousness and irascible behavior became more apparent. My summer trips with him ended when I was twenty-two. After a trip to Disneyworld one August, I had to take a Greyhound bus back home to Massachusetts because he got upset over some innocuous event. I did not hear from him again until I bumped into him at my paternal grandmother's place on Christmas Day four months later. He begrudgingly said, "Hello," as

I was leaving, and he was arriving. Years after she died, my father and I were talking about something that led him to tell me that his doctor thought he was depressed and that he should talk to a professional. My father declared, "I don't need to talk to anybody." I'm not sure what he told his doctor, but I am assuming he said the same exact words to him. He was offended that his doctor had the gall to infer that he had a problem. My father's response is an example of how many people in the Black community respond to mental health issues in their lives, and in the lives of their loved ones. For example, once when I mentioned to my paternal grandmother that I had not heard from my father in a long while, she said something to the effect of, "Don't mind him. You know your father . . . he is probably in one of his moods." I believe this response reflects the prevailing attitude in our community. We often desire to deny reality by adopting a "this too shall pass" mentality. Well, I am now in my forties, and my father is still the same.

Through exploring my own issues surrounding the breakup and how my childhood could have influenced it, I believe that my father's behavior was more characteristic of a personality disorder than simply "moodiness." He presented as someone with many of the characteristics of someone with paranoid personality disorder, which the *Diagnostic and Statistical Manual of Mental Disorders* (DSM-5) describes as:

> A pervasive distrust and suspiciousness of others such that their motives are interpreted as malevolent, beginning by early childhood and present in a variety of contexts, as indicated by four (or more) of the following:
>
> 1. Suspects, without sufficient basis, that others are exploiting, harming, or deceiving him or her.
> 2. Is preoccupied with unjustified doubts about the loyalty or trustworthiness of friends or associates.
> 3. Is reluctant to confide in others because of unwarranted fear that the information will be used maliciously against him or her.
> 4. Reads hidden demeaning or threatening meanings into benign remarks or events.
> 5. Persistently bears grudges (i.e., is unforgiving of insults, injuries, or slights).
> 6. Perceives attacks on his or her character or reputation that are not apparent to others and is quick to react angrily or to counterattack.
> 7. Has recurrent suspicions, without justification, regarding fidelity of spouse or sexual partner. (p. 649)

About two years ago, my father shared a memory of his childhood in the West Indies, where he sometimes had to walk to school barefoot or with cardboard in the bottom of his shoes because of worn soles; and he also mentioned how strict my grandmother was on him. Seventy years later, the memory still seemed to upset him. That same year, my mother described having a mother who was very strict and stern. I can't change the past or my parents, but I can assess the damage that was done to me and take the necessary steps to repair it.

I accepted that my ambivalent and avoidant childhood environment contributed to my low level of confidence in my skills and abilities, led me to constantly seek affirmation and confirmation from others and valuing, and made me trust others' opinions and truths above my own. My codependent disposition paired well with Will's narcissism. In the relationship, I thought I was being a mature person by being understanding and making compromises. What I didn't realize was that I was allowing myself to be compromised. My desire to be deemed worthy blinded me to the truth of who he was and had me settling for mediocrity. I thought I was on a two-way street when in fact I had been careening down a dead-end.

I had become deeply invested emotionally, physically, and mentally in a man that did not exist. Sadly, instead of being relieved that I had been spared, I continued to lament the loss and to wallow in mental anguish, asking myself why I was no longer worthy of his love and commitment? The intensity of my emotions immediately made sense when I discovered that I was going through "abandonment depression," which Masterson describes as "a deep and prolonged despair that produces powerful feelings of abandonment, depression, fear, helplessness, and emptiness that is rooted in your earliest experiences with emotional abandonment" (as cited in Sussman, 2011, p. 196). Because of the unresolved "emotional abandonment" (p. 194) of my parents, I had a void in me that I didn't feel could ever be filled. When Will came into my life, the void was temporarily gone. Then after the relationship ended, I experienced "double abandonment" (p. 196). The void became exponentially wider, and whatever coping tactics my mind had developed to shield me were no longer effective. All the painful emotions were raw, resuscitated, and rejuvenated.

After reading Sussman's (2011) book and going through therapy, I realized that Will was a symptom of my "disease." He was able to fester in my life because of my psychological deficiencies. I didn't know much about his childhood, so I cannot speculate on the full impact his childhood had on him; however, based on what I observed and what he said, I speculate that Will has a narcissistic personality disorder, which is described in the DSM-5 (APA, 2013) as:

> A pervasive pattern of grandiosity (in fantasy or behavior), need for admiration, and lack of empathy, beginning by early adulthood and present in a variety of contexts, as indicated by five (or more) of the following:
>
> 1. Has a grandiose sense of self-importance (e.g., exaggerates achievements and talents, expects to be recognized as superior without commensurate achievements).

2. Is preoccupied with fantasies of unlimited success, power, brilliance, beauty, or ideal love.
3. Believes that he or she is "special" and unique and can only be understood by, or should associate with, other special or high-status people (or institutions).
4. Requires excessive admiration.
5. Has a sense of entitlement (i.e., unreasonable expectations of especially favorable treatment or automatic compliance with his or her expectations).
6. Is interpersonally exploitive (i.e., takes advantage of others to achieve his or her own ends).
7. Lacks empathy: is unwilling to recognize or identify with the feelings and needs of others.
8. Is often envious of others or believes that others are envious of him or her.
9. Shows arrogant, haughty behaviors or attitudes. (p. 669)

Even though Will presented with most of the characteristics and behaviors described above, what impacted me the most was learning that people with this disorder possess a sense of entitlement, and this "entitlement, combined with a lack of sensitivity to the wants and needs of others, may result in the conscious or unwitting exploitation of others." Further, "They tend to form friendships or romantic relationships only if that person seems likely to advance their purposes or otherwise enhance their self-esteem (APA, DSM-5, 2013, p. 670). Will was a vampire in my life, feeding off my generosity, love, and (misplaced) admiration. I didn't put any demands on him. I settled for whatever he could give me emotionally and mentally, even putting up with his ingratitude. For example, after about a year and a half of having him over for Sunday dinners, he became a food critic. If something wasn't prepared the way he preferred, he would push his plate away or ask me if I wanted it. Sundays became stressful, and instead of not cooking for him anymore, I tried harder.

In the beginning of our relationship, he told me that he had "become emotionally dependent on me for companionship and love," and on several occasions thereafter he said he "needed me." Even though he said that earlier in our relationship, that led me to believe that on some level Will wanted to be who I thought he was, and maybe, who he thought he could become. Hearing him say those words made me feel good. However, knowing what I know now, it should have been a red flag. We both had "mental impairments" that fed off of each other in some way. We were temporarily filling voids in our lives. But, ultimately, he knew that he was ill-equipped and unwilling to emotionally invest in the work that it would take to meet my basic needs. In her book, Wilson (2009) states, "Narcissists are naturally psychologically and emotionally abusive because they have almost no room to accommodate others. Any needs you have, even for basic things like love and affection are experienced as impositions and can bring on hostility and what is called narcissistic rage" (pp. 34–35). I believe that Will ended up resenting me for expecting more from him.

Also, during the breakup speech, he had told me that he had been bullied and that he had said things to me to provoke me just for sport. I started recalling all the conversations we had about his eighteen-year marriage, past relationships, and how he treated me. Maya Angelou said that, "When someone shows you who they are, believe them the first time." Will showed *and* told me directly, indirectly, and repeatedly who he was but my own issues caused me to be blind, deaf, and dumb. Even when he shared a few of his issues, I still wondered why he wanted to end the relationship. I wondered why he couldn't see that I could be the antidote for his healing. Had we stayed together, it would have been a classic case of the blind leading the blind.

The breakup with Will affected me more than the end of my marriage of eight years. In hindsight, I believe that I married my ex-husband because he also temporarily filled the void. In the beginning, he gave me the adoration and devotion that I had never received. Of course, I thought that it was all about love, so I moved five hundred miles away to be with him six months after we met and got married five months after that. I think that if I didn't have a void, I would have taken the time to get to know him better. Years after our divorce, I realized that his behaviors were characteristic of a person with Asperger Syndrome, a development disorder.

A year and a half after my relationship with Will ended, I began a relationship with Paul, whom I met at church. It lasted seventy-five days; seventy-three days too long. During our second conversation, he sounded strange—amped up. It was so disconcerting that I asked him if he was drinking. He said that he wasn't. When I talked to my best friend about it, she said that it was probably nerves, so I let it go. If I trusted my own instincts, I wouldn't have been involved with him. Because of my experience with Will, I had become acutely sensitive to people who might have mental and emotional issues and had developed a lower tolerance for what types of behaviors and treatment I would tolerate.

Paul seemed to be a nice and thoughtful guy, but he had issues that were so deep rooted that he had convinced himself, and me, that he didn't have any. I recall that during our time together, I was an open book about my past and present. However, he would not reciprocate and was often vague about his daily activities and whereabouts. I had been to his house, so I knew he wasn't married. He was adamant about not discussing his mom who had died when he was a young adult or other family matters. In the beginning, he would hold my hand all the time and compliment me excessively. However, weeks later, he stopped. In an attempt to figure out what was going on, I mentioned to him once or twice that I liked when he held my hand, but he ignored my comment and started to talk about something else. At the start of the relationship, he said that he liked to hold hands, and that if he stopped showing me affection, then I would know something was wrong. It was clear that he was intentionally withholding affection and playing some sort of mind game.

In her book, Evans (2010) states the following:

> The Abuser who chooses to withhold feels more in control and more powerful if he can remain distant from his partner and, consequently, keep her at bay and yearning. He may also experience a heightened sense of power if his partner's enthusiasm is dampened by his coldness. He seeks this Power Over in order to protect and defend himself from his own feelings of inadequacy. (p. 170)

Whenever he called me, he would ask, "What's going on?" I thought it was just a casual conversation starter, as Will used to ask the same thing. It wasn't until our final conversation, that I learned his greeting was not casual. For some reason, he was insecure about something and was always thinking that more was being said or done than met the eye. I was experiencing a lot of angst in such a short amount of time for no reason at all. Like my father, Paul seemed to exhibit some characteristics of paranoid personality disorder. In addition, I was shocked to realize that I was being verbally abused, which Evans states is unpredictable, insidious, manipulative, and controlling, and expresses a double message. For example, a person might say, "'I am not mad' but sounding very angry" (pp. 77–79).

I was once again entering the bowels of dysfunction. The relationship was starting to affect my emotional well-being, and I didn't like how I was allowing him to make me feel—always on edge and unhappy. So, one day when he said, "This is not working," which he had said two or three times before, I did not engage in a discussion to find out what was wrong and to find out what imaginary thing I had said or done. Instead, I said that I had done everything I could and that sometimes things don't work out. He asked if I was agreeing with him, as if he were surprised. I took my chance of escape and said, "Yes." I immediately felt the spirit of peace wash over my body. I was free.

Jewell (1988), Franklin (2011), and McAdoo (2007) are just a few authors who have studied and written extensively about the historic challenges that Black people face. Many of these studies have focused on how discrimination; socioeconomics; demographics; educational disparities; cultural changes; housing issues; health; and poverty have negatively impacted Black people and, by extension, Black families. Even though we have made great strides, I believe those issues, in addition to genetics, still contribute to the state of our emotional and mental well-being. Moreover, we must realize that for people of color, especially Black people, there is a preponderance of evidence that shows that the same resources extended for nonpersons of color are not available to us. For example, the media often disproportionally uses pejorative stereotypes to label Black men as being dangerous, aggressive, and animalistic; and Black women as being angry, aggressive, ill tempered, illogical, overbearing, and hostile without mentioning the possibility of mental impairment. In turn, Black men are readily jailed or killed, intentionally or not, with no chance for substantive mental evaluation and treatment, whereas a White person is often quickly labeled as mentally unstable, thereby eliciting sympathy and understanding instead of fear and loathing. Given these issues and practices, it is understandable how our mental health could be further impacted negatively.

How many relationship conversations have we heard where the words "crazy" or "has issues" are used to describe a partner. These words are often used to describe unreasonable behavior and perplexing situations and circumstances. Even if we have an inclination that something deeper is afoot, we might be reluctant to voice our concerns. This might be due to our own ignorance about mental health issues, thereby making us unsure of our suspicions. Also, because of the historical and current sociocultural climate, we might not want to get law enforcement or medical professionals involved or risk the chance of our partner or oneself being ostracized by family and friends. Mental illness can lead to job loss, relationship breakdowns, or the disintegration of life as we know it. We must remember that "change" is not a bad word.

In my case, I was aware of the oft signaled statistics of fewer viable Black men than Black women in the dating pool, which is one of the reasons that made me fearful of starting over again. Despite encouragement from friends and access to spiritual and inspirational messages reassuring that I would recover and find love again, my faith was challenged on a daily basis. My natural and healthy inclination to figure out what was wrong with me delayed the healing process, because in doing so, I usually shouldered all the responsibility for the relationship ending. I did not entertain the possibility that the relationship had simply run its course, etc. However, through therapy and reading, my journey of self-exploration began in earnest. I realized that my father, Will, and Paul were working with the hand that they had been dealt. Some of us are better card players than others and some of us don't know how to play at all. I don't excuse them for treating me the way that they did, but, as the saying goes, "hurt people, hurt people." I wish Paul and Will the best and hope that they find peace. My only goal is not to let my past hurts negatively affect my future relationships.

It took me thirty years to realize that my parents were incapable of being who I thought they should be and that they lacked the self-awareness and tools to do so. I don't know everything that they went through, but I now know enough to let them off the hook, and I have started the process of

accepting them for who they are and forgiving them and forgiving myself for
not valuing myself more and not loving myself—regardless.

The National Alliance of Mental Illness (NAMI) cites the Health and
Human Services Office of Minority Health's claim that African Americans
are 20 percent more likely to experience serious mental health problems than
other groups. So, even though slavery has been abolished, I contend that
when it comes to the issue of mental health, many in our community are still
enslaved emotionally, and freedom can only be achieved when the stigma of
having a mental disorder is stymied. The good news is that in recent years,
strides have been made and progress is continuing, especially in the entertainment world, where celebrities, such as Mariah Carey, Jenifer Lewis, and
DMX, have detailed their personal struggles with mental health.

In addition, the increase of mental health disorders among millennials
might also further bring the topic of mental health in the Black community to
the forefront. According to the article, poor mental health among millennials
is at an all-time high, and among this demographic, mental health issues have
tripled in the last few years (Open Access Government, 2018). Further,
young adults: . . . are considered an anxious generation, which is often
attributed to an obsession with technology, overbearing parents, and the
stress that comes with trying to fit into a social media-driven world. But,
according to experts, the anxiety and depression often experienced by these
young adults lies in uncertainty about future careers, parental pressures to
succeed, low self-esteem and self-image issues in the age of social media,
and FOMO—the fear of missing out (p. 1).

Official statistics all provide alarming numbers:

- 1,180 students left university in early 2014–2015 due to mental health
  problems
- 50 percent of mental health problems occur by the age of fourteen and 75
  percent by age twenty-four
- Almost five times as many students suffer from a mental health condition
  compared to ten years ago
- More than 15,000 students in the UK disclosed a mental health issue in
  2015–2016, compared to 3,000 in 2006
- 87,914 students requested counseling in 2015–2016, a 28 percent rise
  from 2013–2014
- In 2015, 2.5 percent of female students and 1.4 percent of male students
  disclosed a mental health issue compared to 0.5 percent for both sexes in
  2009–2010.

These UK statistics reveal how universal the issue of mental health is, and
that it's not just a US problem, not just a problem for a particular race,
ethnicity, or culture. However, if mental health is having such a widespread

and encompassing effect on all groups, I contend that based on the history of Black people aforementioned and as examined by Jewell (1988), Franklin (2011), and McAdoo (2007), then there must be more of us hiding our issues.

I believe that with more celebrities sharing their struggles, more media attention, more research, more available community resources, and more outreach from places of worship, myths about mental health in the Black community will decrease, and, hopefully, meaningful conversations will extend beyond what's happening in Hollywood or in books but into our homes and communities. Having mental and emotional issues is not weakness and seeking help takes courage and strength. Taking advantage of all available resources will empower us and enable us to regain control over our lives. Our childhood, how we were raised, heredity, societal pressures, and our previous/current environment only keep us bound and cause us to succumb to oppressive limits and to deny our destiny. We need to break the cycle of silence, avoidance, fear of exposure, and inertia that supersede our need for help. Further, as a mother of a nonverbal young adult who has significant cognitive delays and a seizure disorder, I cannot afford the cost of silence. My life and her well-being depend on me being mentally and emotionally healthy. My role as a parent must supersede my desire to keep up appearances. As it states in the Bible, "For God hath not given us the spirit of fear; but of power, and of love, and of a sound mind" (2 Timothy 1:7, KJV).

REFERENCES

American Psychological Association. (2013). *American Psychological Association: Diagnostic and Statistical Manual of Mental Disorders (5th ed.)*. Arlington, VA: American Psychological Association.

Bernstein, A. (2012). *Emotional Vampires: Dealing with People Who Drain You Dry (2nd ed.)*. New York: McGraw-Hill.

Evans, P. (2010). *The Verbally Abusive Relationship: How to Recognize It and How to Respond (3rd ed.)*. Avon, MA: Adams Media.

Franklin, J. H. (2011). *From Slavery to Freedom: A History of African Americans (9th ed.)*. New York: McGraw Hill.

Jewell, K. S. (1988). *Survival of the Black Family*. Westport, CT: Praeger.

Kübler-Ross, E., and Kessler, D. (2005). *On Grief and Grieving: Finding the Meaning of Grief Through the Five Stages of Loss*. New York: Scribner.

McAdoo, H. P. (2007). *Black Families (4th ed.)*. Thousand Oaks, CA: Sage Publications.

Open Access Government. (2018, October 11). "Mental Health among Millennials at All Time High," Retrieved January 25, 2019, from https://www.openaccessgovernment.org/mental-health-among-millennials/53137/

Sussman, R. (2011). *The Breakup Bible*. New York: Three Rivers Press.

Wilson, B. (2009). *He's Just No Good for You: A Guide to Getting Out of a Destructive Relationship*. Guilford, CT: The Globe Pequot Press.

Chapter Nine

Between an African American and Trinidadian

An Autoethnography of Race, Identity, and Love

Renata Ferdinand

I often tell my students of how I met my husband.

It was 2006 in Columbus, Ohio. I was a graduate student at Bowling Green State University, about two hours from Columbus, but I happened to be in the area to attend a Junior Reid concert. My friends and I were so excited for this reggae concert in particular, especially as we were huge fans of the "One Love" artist.

I had especially dressed for the occasion. I retwisted my locks, put on a new dress, and topped it off with a pair of glass slippers. I walked—no strutted—into the club with unabashed confidence.

That's when I saw him. Actually, I saw his milk chocolate skin before I saw anything else. His perfect hue was only enhanced by the locks he wore up in a high bun. He was smooth, and he knew it. I gawked at this man as he majestically danced across the floor, everyone captivated by his moving body.

I attempted to make eye contact with him but he never responded.

I did all sorts of things. I stood provocatively so he could see me, to no avail. I inched closer so he could see my gorgeous glass slippers, still nothing. I made sure he noticed the men that I had rejected when they offered to buy me drinks. He just didn't care.

I spent so much of my time in that club trying to get this man's attention, I didn't get to fully enjoy the performance by Junior Reid. When the musician finished his last song, I waited until the lights were completely turned on to see if I could, at the very least, meet the artist.

And that's when it happened. The man I had nearly stalked all night was helping Junior Reid and his band disassemble their set. I knew I had to strike!

I walked over to him confident and reassured that if he rejected me there was something particularly wrong with him. My five foot four stance came about halfway to his broad six foot frame. Yet, I didn't care. I uttered the words that seem infamous now in Black dating relationships, "hey boo." That was thirteen years ago. Since that fateful meeting, we got married, had two kids, and moved to Brooklyn, New York.

I have learned many things along this journey. When I was eyeing this man, I did not know that he was from the Caribbean, Trinidad and Tobago in particular. And as an African American woman who had never dated someone from the islands, I had no idea of how our specific cultural background would affect the dynamics of our relationship. But it did, and it continues to this very day.

I look at Black relationships and I think about my own. Not only is my particular relationship impacted by cultural background, it is also affected by it simply being a Black relationship. Black relationships in the United States are met with alarming statistics that point to the lack of stable marriages that often contribute to a cycle of single parenthood, among other things, within Black families. Much of this is documented in the research. But what is less often explored is the reasons for this phenomenon, particularly the sociocultural pressures that are largely ignored in an examination of Black relationships.

Hence, this gives me a reason to write, especially as the lack of anecdotal, experiential, and personal exploration of this topic buttresses hegemonic discussions of relationships and marriages, which often exclude the voices of persons of African descent. Taylor et al. (2012) write that "very little research examines marital and romantic relationship quality and satisfaction among African Americans and even less focuses on Black Caribbeans" (p. 374). I aim to close this glaring gap by using my own intimate partner relationship to reveal the intimacies and intricacies of Black love.

This is an autoethnography. Denzin and Lincoln (1997) explain autoethnography best:

> Autoethnography is setting a scene, telling a story, weaving intricate connections among life and art, experience and theory, evocation and explanation . . . and then letting it go, hoping for readers who will bring the same careful attention to your words in the context of their own lives. (p. 208)

Specifically, this essay provides an intimate look at the societal influences that have affected my thirteen-year relationship with my husband. As an autoethnography, it brings forth that which is often lost within theory and empirical data by using the relationship between my husband and I to expose the ways in which sociocultural pressures affect Black relationships. In the midst of countless barriers and hurdles, I contend that three important factors have emerged as confounding influences on our relationship, which have led to undue pressure and stress: differences in cultural background, exposure and experience with US racism and discrimination, and the role of a shared Black identity. I believe that exploring these particular factors as they relate to Black relationships will reveal a very complex dynamic and maybe offer a more nuanced way of understanding the subtle, yet insidious circumstances that lead to failed Black relationships.

She saw the building in plain sight.

We moved a lot during the course of our relationship. Early in our marriage, we moved back to my home state of Georgia. Georgia was never a fixed structure in my mind. I never longed for it or reminisced about it when I lived elsewhere. In fact, I had no reservations or hesitations when I moved alone to Bowling Green to complete my master's degree, or when I stayed to complete a doctorate. And during that time, I spent summers studying abroad in West Africa, including Burkina Faso, Ghana, Benin, and Togo. Georgia was the last thing on my mind.

But I did appreciate certain experiences, like visiting Dr. Martin Luther King, Jr.'s monument in Atlanta. Or seeing the remnants of the Macon bus boycott, in which my father participated in downtown Macon. Or participating in Juneteenth Celebrations or Kwanzaa events at the local parks. From the plantations to the historic Black neighborhoods, Georgia offered a piece of celebratory Black history that remained pivotal to my Black identity.

But it wasn't this piece of history that my husband admired about Georgia. He loved the lifestyle—the easiness of what he perceived to be a Georgia life. He loved how friendly people were, how they would so easily converse with strangers. He loved how the pace of life was slower—no one seemed to honk horns in a frantic rush to get to anywhere. And he loved the weather. The months of summer on end with only two months of winter somewhat reminded him of his childhood growing up in Trinidad. And most of all, he loved living around my family. It was these things he loved, not so much the blackness of the location. Although he was surrounded by African American culture, he gravitated to those things not specifically Black. In the beginning of our marriage, our differences were emerging.

I knew what being African American meant to me, and the way Black culture had impacted my identity, and my life in general. Joseph and colleagues (2013) explain:

> African American culture is said to have emerged within a distinct history of
> racial oppression, including post-emancipation racial discrimination and vio-

lence. As a result, although African American culture is not solely based on oppression, it contains a distinct narrative around racial struggle and uplift. (p. 415)

This understanding has guided my perspective. I stressed Black heritage and culture in almost everything I did, as African American culture "blends West African cosmologies, including an emphasis on spirituality, orality, and harmony with others with cultural traditions and practices of European/American society" (Joseph et al., 2013, p. 414). As a professor of English and African American Studies, I taught this in my courses. I volunteered in local organizations to help sustain it. Justice and equality became significant themes in my household. But this was largely due to my insistence, not so much from my husband.

My husband emphasized his Trinidadian identity. I wore shirts that represented his country. He carried a Trinidadian flag in his back pocket, and even bought seat covers with the Trinidad and Tobago emblem emblazoned on it. When he visited home, he brought back items to decorate our home with—from pictures and statues to a keyholder and pen case. Trinidad was everywhere.

It was then that I began to truly understand our differences. Here I was, so rooted in my African American identity, which centered on blackness, racial uplift, and empowerment. And yet, I was married to a man that emphasized a particular ethnic identity. Foner (2016) describes Caribbean immigrants as "often assert[ing] an ethnic identity as natives of a particular Caribbean island or as West Indians more generally" (p. 65). Clearly, we were different. Johnson (2016) describes how Black immigrant's historical experience of colonialism and empire differs from Black American history of racial subjugation, which "permeated black America and created among its members as a group an oppositional consciousness that continues to serve as a tool to face the enduring challenges of a deeply race-based society" (p. 55). I wish my husband was more like Barbara Ceptus, who Johnson describes as having learned ways to merge her Haitian identity with a Black identity despite the dismay of her parents and grandparents who identify as Haitian only.

Needless to say, this influenced and impacted our interactions with our children. I saw this when my husband questioned my teaching our children about Kwanzaa, or the endless questions he would ask when I lectured my daughter about African traditional religions like Yoruba. He would listen attentively as I showed my daughter pictures of the slave dungeons of Elmina and Cape Coast Castle in Ghana. He never failed to recognize the little Black boy books I would buy for my son. He might have even secretly objected to my insistence that he return any toys given as gifts to our children if they were not Black, but he never said anything.

But what he did say often focused on his immigrant experience. He regaled our children with his hardships growing up in Trinidad, often lacking food and electricity. He told them how he started working at five-years-old, abruptly ending his childhood to help support his family of six. He demonstrated how he would carve wood sculptures and then try to peddle them to the European visitors to Port of Spain. He stressed the importance of water, how he often bathed only when it rained, or when he and his friends would venture to the beach. To this day, he often remembers the feeling of being thirsty and hungry.

This is how the beginning of our marriage took shape. We were like most couples, finding the ebb and flow of our relationship. But our particular cultural background, mine rooted in race and his in an immigrant identity, managed to influence our day-to-day lives. It would take us time to figure out this dynamic. And as we did, we continued to move, first around Georgia, then to Potsdam, New York.

She saw the blinking sign.

I had never even heard of Potsdam. I had trouble finding it on a map of New York. But there it was, in Upstate New York, nestled between Canton, New York, and Canada. In fact, it was about thirty-four miles from the Canadian border. Once I saw the location, I knew there would hardly be any Black people there. But I didn't deter. I had a new job opportunity and I was hoping that this move would secure my footing as an assistant professor.

My husband had no qualms about moving. Even though he loved Georgia, he also appreciated and understood the significance of moving for better economic and job opportunities. I suspect that had I suggested this idea to an African American man, this might have played out very differently, simply because African Americans tend to live in or near major metropolitan areas, places where Black culture is easily accessible. It is more likely that my husband's immigrant identity led him to agree to this move, having left home and emigrated here in 1997 to New York City, then to Ohio. Taylor and colleagues (2012) suggest that the dynamics created by the immigrant experience of Black Caribbeans makes Black family dynamics more fluid, as "by virtue of migration, Black Caribbeans [families] are much more geographically dispersed than African American families. Many Black Caribbean families are transnational; it is common for relatives to reside in locations as dispersed as Brooklyn, New York, London, and Montreal, as well as their country of origin" (p. 384). So, we left Georgia with high hopes.

But those hopes were quickly dashed when we realized where we were. In this picturesque town with rolling green hills and quaint downtown shops lay a hidden ugliness: racism. It slowly but surely revealed itself in day-to-day interactions, from our being blatantly, and clumsily, I might add, followed in

Walmart to my daughter's pre-K teacher's admonishment to me that the other children's parents were not ready for a Black child in the classroom, and that I couldn't force people to accept this. It revealed itself when my husband applied for jobs, with one potential employer asking him, "What color are you?" It reared its ugly head at my job too, when professors often complained of the New York City kids who came to school there, even though most of the raucous caused on campus and in the town were from local kids. It was everywhere. But the tipping point came in another way.

We often took trips to New York City, which was about six hours away, to get away from this environment. One day, after loading our things into the car, we began the long drive down the isolated roads. But on our way out of town, the road normally deserted and quiet was buzzing with activity. It was only as we reached closer that we saw the road block policed by the border agents. My heart jumped in my throat.

We both sat cautiously in our seat as we came upon the road block. My husband rolled down the window as one agent approached his window, the other approached mine. I sat quietly but slowly turned to look at my then four-year-old daughter fast asleep in the backseat.

The agent asked my husband for his license and registration, which he gladly handed over. The agent then asked our purpose in the area. When my husband responded that I was a professor at SUNY Canton, the agent leaned in closer, not to look at me but to hear my husband better. He wasn't so much shocked at what he said; instead, he was shocked by my husband's accent. He immediately instructed for my husband and I to get out of the car.

I sat on the curb trying to answer all the questions the officer had about my employment while the other one searched my husband. He patted him down for weapons. He asked him for his particular reason for being here, as if being a husband was not a valid reason for being with his wife who worked in the area. He asked his home country, how long he lived in the United States, and his permanent resident status. My husband answered all of these questions with no problem.

But then came the dogs. The agents strolled back to their vehicles and brought out two vicious canines. They proceeded to search our car, with the dogs sniffing around the tires and inside the trunk. They sniffed up and down my husband's body. We were on display; while all of this took place, cars slowly drove by. Passersby pointed, sneered, some of them even laughed. I was beyond broken. I cannot recall how long this episode lasted, could have been a few minutes, could have been an hour. By the time it was completely over and the agents said we could leave, I boiled in anger, on the verge of rage. I felt like Griffin (2012):

> I AM an Angry Black Woman. Unapologetically, rationally, and rightfully so.
> I am blistering mad! I am frustrated and enraged! I am devastated, and my

> blood is boiling at a temperature so hot that I think my heart might stop beating at any given moment. (p. 138)

Thankfully, my daughter slept through this entire scene. But I couldn't rest. But neither could I adequately articulate myself. I didn't know what to say. I, the English professor, couldn't find the words. And neither could he. We drove to New York City in silence, a six-hour drive with no words.

By the time we made it to New York City, we were emotionally heavy. We carried it with us the entire journey. I can't remember if he got angry with me or I with him, but we argued as soon as we hit the city. It was over something so stupid, like where we were going to stop and eat. Yet that wasn't really the argument. The argument was really about what happened Upstate. It just came out over burgers and fries.

When we did finally have a conversation about it a few days later, a statement my husband made brought my anger from the back to the forefront. When I tried expressing the racial elements of the story, he quickly stopped me and said, "Well, we live near the border, so they likely did this because of that. It just happened because of that." I stood quiet, now angry at him.

I began to ramble off the wrongness of the situation, that if race was not a factor, then why were we the only ones who "just happened" to be put under that type of scrutiny? Would someone with a British accent or Russian accent be subjected to that line of inquiry about their status? The dogs reminded me of the Civil Rights Era, when they were used as enforcers to brutalize Black bodies simply asking to be treated with basic human dignity. I tried reminding him that police agents and Black people have a tumultuous relationship grounded in historical factors, just as Brooks et al. (2016) write, "Law enforcement is still an oppressive force for Black men. Throughout the Civil Rights Era (1950s–1960s), law enforcement was utilized to enforce and restrict Black rights, as well as use of public facilities enjoyed by White counterparts" (p. 349). But my husband didn't know this history. And this was before the public execution of Black males like Travyon Martin, Michael Brown, and Eric Garner. I think he was not quick to accept that "the fear of Black males can make life dangerous for Black men. Indeed, reported data strongly suggests that Black males are the most discriminated group by the police" (Brooks et al., 2016, p. 354). I said all of this but he was unmoved.

Undoubtedly, I began to look at him differently. Not right or wrong, just different. And I began to question whether I could accurately trust his judgment on certain things. I wasn't sure. I thought to myself that if he couldn't see this situation for what it was, then how could I count on him to view anything accurately, especially things so glaringly in front of his eyes? For a moment, the dynamics of our relationship changed for the worse. Abrams, Maxwell, and Belgrave (2018) cite their study as well as previous research that demonstrates that "racism and discrimination . . . [are] reasons for poor relationship quality between Black men and women" (p. 158). In this moment, I knew this statement to be true.

And then we moved again. Actually, the racial climate was so tense in this environment that six months later we moved to Brooklyn, New York.

She knew they were entering through the wrong way.

I never had any desire to live in New York City. It was never a long-awaited dream of mine. I never even wished to visit it. But when the situation Upstate became too toxic, I applied to jobs in the closest vicinity. Only the ones in the city answered my call. So, we packed up and moved to New York City, specifically, Brooklyn. My husband took the lead on this as he had lived here before.

New York City is surprisingly segregated. I only found this out after moving here—I thought racial segregation was a relic from the South, from my home in Georgia. Yet, it was here that I learned the staunch anti-desegregation efforts that occurred, like the fifteen thousand White mothers who marched from the Brooklyn Bridge to City Hall in Manhattan in 1964 to protest school busing policies. Delmont (2016) writes, "By calling themselves Parents and Taxpayers, these white protestors made an implicit claim that they occupied a higher level of citizenship than black and Puerto Rican New Yorkers, who were also parents and taxpayers" (p. 8). Now that's the New York that's not advertised, the one that Purnell and Theoharis (2017) dub the "capital of the Jim Crow North."

We settled into the vibrant East Flatbush neighborhood. At the time, I didn't know that East Flatbush was home to one of the largest Caribbean neighborhoods in New York City, with over 50 percent of the population being from a foreign country. I didn't know that my choicest of culinary delights would likely be a Jamaican beef patty or roti from the Trinidad and Tobago shop. I didn't know that the market shelves would be stocked with exotic fruits and vegetables that I had never even heard of, let alone seen. But my husband knew this. As it happens, we came to live just ten minutes away from his old apartment.

This new move created a different reality for me. In this environment, I was the foreigner. In my immediate surroundings, I was always the only African American. I had trouble discerning accents. I struggled to communicate with shopkeepers, restaurant workers, teachers, you name it. My southern accent became a thing to admire here. I recall the countless times that I have been stopped midsentence just so someone can know what part of the South I am from. It actually became a running joke in my house.

Here, in East Flatbush, Caribbean people ran the show—it was in the colors of flags waving from houses, in the stilt walkers that sauntered down

the street practicing for West Indian Day Parade, in the home-country independence celebrations that brought a diversity of peoples and the blaring of
music.

And I began to learn of a new dimension to my husband. I saw him in an
environment that was essentially his home. He felt comfortable here, had a
plethora of friends, and took life here to be like life in Trinidad. He began to
play more soca and reggae music. He brought home native foods like calla-
loo and roti skin. He ate doubles from the Trinidad and Tobago food truck.
This was the first time I'd seen him like this. He almost appeared like someone new to me. He used words I didn't understand. His accent even got
thicker! Foner (2016) writes, "West Indian identity is nurtured and reinforced
among [those] who grow up and continue to live in neighborhoods with a
critical mass of Afro-Caribbeans" (p. 65). Who was this guy?

It seemed like when in Georgia, he was more willing to acquiesce to
African American culture even if he did not have a deep appreciation for it.
But here, he didn't have to do this. Joseph et al. (2013) finds that "when
Black Caribbean-descended individuals believe that the public perceives
their ethnic group positively they are less engaged in African American
culture" (p. 420). Here, in this Caribbean enclave, it was great to be Caribbean.

I also noticed that my husband treated his friends more like family. My
husband's friends became a significant part of his life. He often talked of
how they grew up together in Trinidad, and when he emigrated here, they
helped him settle and learn the customs of the United States. In fact, his
friends and I seemed to share the same level of importance. I realized this one
day when I noticed that he phoned them and I each day before leaving work.
I recall one particular argument over this.

I had asked him to not attend a party with them and to instead, spend time
with me. But he hesitated to give me a response. Clearly, he wanted to check
in with them first before providing me with an answer. I watched his face
when he finally spoke with them on the phone—a sheer look of disappointment. Yet his disappointment was not due to his eagerness to go to the party;
rather, it was because he didn't want to disappoint them. In weighing his
options of who to disappoint, he chose me and left to go to the party.

We argued and argued. Somewhere in the midst of the argument I told my
husband about how his new behavior was troubling to me, how I no longer
felt important in his life, that now I was competing as a wife with his friends.
And he responded with a shocking comment: "I need my friends. Just in case
you decide to leave me one day, I'll have a back-up plan and won't be left in
this country alone."

I couldn't believe it. Again, I was at a loss for words. Here I was, standing
in front of a man that I had, at this time, been married to for seven years. And
all I heard was, "you are not important, you are not important, you are not

important." Our relationship was in trouble. I was a foreigner in my relationship with him.

We stayed in this spiral for a while to the point where I considered leaving the marriage. It's crazy how situations can change relationships—I had lived in different environments with this man but it was only when we lived in this Caribbean one that I thought of throwing in the towel. Love was only one thing that stopped me—the other was the stereotype of the broken Black family. I didn't want to be a single mother, nor did I want to be one of those African Americans who "spend less time in marriage than whites" (Taylor et al., 2012, p. 375). I knew my family wasn't like the one depicted on *The Cosby Show*, but I, like many other African Americans, longed to exhibit the traits of this intact, nuclear functional family. I was just like Steve in Perry, Smith, and Brooms (2014) study who watched the show, which, "though fictional, represented a long-term committed relationship and fostered Steve's desire to experience such commitment in his own marriage" (p. 491). I looked at a show like *Black Love* on OWN and tried to maintain my steadfast approach. So, I stayed and figured out how to make this work.

It was only in the staying that I learned other things about my marriage, and more so, about my husband's immigrant identity. I tried to be more involved in his island life. This included me learning how to buy and fill barrels with all sorts of goodies, from flat screen televisions to clothing items and household goods, to send to his family in Trinidad. I learned the importance of the Caribbean mobile phone carrier Digicel, of sending money through Western Union, and of acquiring items to be sent back home with traveling friends. Taylor and colleagues (2012) explains:

> [the] Migration process involves behaviors and strategies that sustain family ties across households (i.e., remittances and financial exchanges). These adaptive economic (i.e., social network ties) and psychological (i.e., immigrant ethic and achievement orientation) strategies effectively buffer the hardships associated with immigration. (p. 384)

It seemed we were both now caught in this process.

I also tried inviting his friends over more, and conversely, attending their gatherings. And in this environment, I came to learn more about them as a people, and especially, their thought processes. They, too, accepted each other as family—foreigners in a foreign land who are making it in America together. They relied on each other for financial, social, and emotional support. Wilson (2009) writes, "First, continued communication to and from home/family following migration, as well as community building with others from the region, allowed immigrants to use the family/home connections as socio-cultural resources to mitigate adjustment" (p. 199). I saw this as they volunteered to babysit for each other, loaned each other their cars, and threw celebratory parties for each other's achievements.

And when I voiced my fears of Trump, and especially of the Charlottesville Riot that occurred on August 11 and 12 of 2017, and our need to maybe leave this country before it imploded, they adamantly met my request with caution, admitting that they would never leave this country. Johnson (2016) cites Robinson's (2010) book *Disintegration: The Splintering of Black America*: "Immigrants [black immigrants from Africa and the Caribbean] may have complicated feelings about the European colonial powers, but America is seen as an imperfect society that nevertheless offers economic opportunity and political freedom" (p. 31). I was seeing this firsthand.

They rambled on and on about their permanent residence status. When I questioned them on why they loved this country so much but never became a citizen, they mostly all responded in unison that becoming a natural citizen was not an option. They responded in the way that Wilson (2009) writes: "To remain a permanent resident allows one the flexibility of saying, 'I am from the Caribbean, but I live and work in the United States,' versus, 'I am an American citizen, but I grew up in the Caribbean'" (p. 202). I would have initially taken this as indifference or a plain lack of knowledge regarding the extent of racial problems in the United States, but this taught me another perspective.

It was love there.

So, we began to work on our relationship, and I realized that what I perceived as his dismissiveness of me was actually something larger operating as a function of his immigrant identity. The connections he has established here helped to ground him in this country. Yet, I also knew that he had already made a difficult separation from his parents and siblings in Trinidad to come here. So, it was not that he didn't care about me; he just had to refigure me into his immigrant dream.

She said nothing.

I am the "she" described in the short sentences throughout this essay. What I am describing is the scene of arriving to the hospital to give birth to my son. My husband was so excited! I've learned that in his excitement he sometimes loses his senses. In this case, he lost his sense of direction and had us entering through the wrong door. Hospital personnel had to stop us and redirect us to the correct entrance.

But what is even more startling is that I knew that we were going through the wrong entrance. I knew simply because I was a bit more familiar with the hospital than he was. But I said nothing. I allowed him to lead us down the wrong path even though my water had broken and I had begun active labor.

My mother is still astonished as why I would do that. She asked, "You would follow this man over a cliff as well?"

I think now about why I did that. I think I did that for his manhood more so than anything else. I think I may have been responding in the way that has been found in the research about Black women. Research shows how Black women assume more traditional gendered characteristics to compensate for how Black men are treated in larger society. A participant in Cowdery's et al. (2009) study responded that she gladly let her husband assume a powerful role, "cause no man, no Black man wants a wife, a woman, who knows more than he does" (p. 32). I guess, in some ways, I subscribed to this idea. Actually, this says more about me than it does him because I don't know if he even subscribed to or paid attention to the role of Black men in society but I sure did.

So, here I was, an educated Black woman, allowing this to happen. And not just at any moment, but while I was in labor, carrying another life. When I think about it now, it seems so stupid. I was projecting my own historical and contemporary experiences of being Black in this country onto him, thinking that I was filling some hole or void that had been created in his psyche as a Black man. This one, single act, I thought, would be enough to make up for what the world had done to him. I was like the women in Abrams et al.'s (2018) study, which collected Black women's perceptions of Black manhood, finding that the women believed that "limited resources, prejudices, discriminatory practices, incarceration, disadvantages stemming from childhood, internalized stereotypes, and/or a combination of these barriers prevent [Black men from accomplishing goals]" (p. 156). But this didn't happen to my husband, at least not to the extent that it showed in his personality. I really did this for myself, not for him.

Hill-Collins (2004) describes how Black men and women share a common historical bond of racism that has permeated every aspect of Black daily life. But what happens when a Black couple does not share that same bond? Or the circumstances of the bond are very different? Is blackness enough to hold a couple together? And even more pressing, how does a Black couple who don't share the same historical experience navigate a successful relationship? Admittedly, I don't know the answers to these questions for I'm still figuring much of this out myself. I do know that some things are a bit easier with me having an immigrant husband—I can move states effortlessly, switch religions, change and wildly grow, and expose my kids to different cultures and different ways of thinking and viewing life. And yet, some things are a bit difficult—the different historical experiences that have influenced us both and dictated our contemporary life, the language barrier that sometimes complicates our ability to communicate clearly, and, in general, a lack of cultural understanding. Things are not perfect. But just like other relationships, it takes a little flair, creativity, patience, and understanding.

And we are still together.

REFERENCES

Abrams, J., Maxwell, M., & Belgrave, F. (2018). "Circumstances Beyond Their Control: Black Women's Perceptions of Black Manhood." *Sex Roles, 79*, 151–62.

Brooks, M., Ward, C., Euring, M., Townsend, C., White, N., & Hughes, K. (2016). "Is There a Problem Officer? Exploring the Lived Experience of Black Men and Their Relationship with Law Enforcement." *Journal of African American Studies, 20*, 346–62.

Cowdery, R. S., Scarborough, N., Knudson-Martin, C., Seshadri, G., Lewis, M. E., & Mahoney, A. R. (2009). "Gendered Power in Cultural Contexts: Part II. Middle Class African American Heterosexual Couples with Young Children." *Family Process, 48*(1), 25–39.

Delmont, M. (2016, Oct. 4). "The Origins of 'Antibusing' Politics: New York City Protests and Revision of the Civil Rights Act." Retrieved from https://www.gothamcenter.org/blog/the-origins-of-antibusing-politics-new-york-city-protests-and-revision-of-the-civil-rights-act

Denzin, N., & Lincoln, Y. (1997). *Collecting and Interpreting Qualitative Materials.* Thousand Oaks, CA: Sage.

Foner, N. (2016). "Black Immigrants and the Realities of Racism: Comments and Questions." *Journal of American Ethnic History, 36*(1), 63–70.

Griffin, R. (2012). "I Am an Angry Black Woman: Black Feminist Autoethnography, Voice, and Resistance." *Women's Studies in Communication, 35*(2), 138–57.

Hill-Collins, P. (2004). *Black Sexual Politics: African Americans, Gender, and the New Racism.* New York: Routledge.

Johnson, V. S. (2016). "When Blackness Stings: African and Afro-Caribbean Immigrants, Race, and Racism in Late Twentieth-Century America." *Journal of American Ethnic History, 36*(1), 31–62.

Joseph, N., Watson, N., Wang, Z., Case, A., & Hunter, C. (2013). "Rules of Engagement: Predictors of Black Caribbean Immigrants' Engagement with African American Culture." *Cultural Diversity and Ethnic Minority Psychology, 19*(4), 414–23.

Perry, A., Smith, S., & Brooms, D. (2014). "'You Ain't No Denzel': African American Men's Use of Popular Culture to Narrate and Understand Marriage and Romantic Relationships." *Journal of African American Studies, 18*, 485–97.

Purnell, B., & Theoharis, J. (2017, August 23). "How New York City Became the Capital of the Jim Crow North." *The Washington Post.* Retrieved from https://www.washingtonpost.com/news/made-by-history/wp/2017/08/23/how-new-york-city-became-the-capital-of-the-jim-crow-north/?noredirect=on&utm_term=.649c7b0059ee

Robinson, E. (2010). *Disintegration: The Splintering of Black America.* New York: Doubleday.

Taylor, R. J., Brown, E., Chatters, L. M., & Lincoln, K. D. (2012). "Extended Family Support and Relationship Satisfaction among Married, Cohabiting, and Romantically-Involved African Americans and Black Caribbeans." *Journal of African American Studies, 16*, 373–89.

Wilson, E. (2009). "What It Means to Become a United States American: Afro-Caribbean Immigrants' Constructions of American Citizenship and Experience of Cultural Transition." *Journal of Ethnographic & Qualitative Research, 3*, 196–204.

Index

About the Editor and Contributors

Tapo Chimbganda, PhD, worked in higher education in Canada and England but her passion has always been strengthening individuals and families through comprehensive strategies that educate, empower, and enlighten people to meet their life goals. Tapo has almost twenty years' experience working for community and non-profit organizations, schools, healthcare providers, and in private practice as a psychoanalytic psychotherapist. She holds professional licenses in Canada and the USA. She has presented at conferences in Australia, Finland, Canada, and other parts of the world; and has been published on matters of mental health, education, the social family, and social justice. Her first book, *The Classroom as Privileged Space*, an academic text published in 2017, focuses on social justice and education for marginalized populations. Tapo is a registered member of the International Association for Relationship Research (IARR). In 2019, she founded a not-for-profit, Future Black Female, geared toward helping Black female youth rise up in all areas of their lives.

ABOUT THE CONTRIBUTORS

Carissa McCray, PhD, has engaged in multiple relationships with religion including participation with both the Nuwaubian Nation and Black Hebrew Israelite. Due to her relationship with both religions, she speaks firsthand of her experiences as a Black woman attempting to find understanding of religion that both uplifts and grounds her. She views herself as an immersive anthropologist with the ability to analyze her experiences constructively without animosity. With diverse lenses and perspectives for analysis, Dr.

McCray plans to add to her writing repertoire various religious experiences from people of color.

Jade Benn is a master's graduate carving out a career as a writer. She has experience working with young women at risk of sexual violence and in formal education. Jade founded a social enterprise in 2016, the Black British Library (on Facebook), which records the experiences of the Black diaspora residing in the UK. Currently, Jade is working on a film, podcasting (The EchoChamber), and writing freelance.

Michael Baugh is an instructor and education program specialist at Georgia Southern University. Currently ABD, he seeks a doctorate in curriculum studies at Georgia Southern. Michael received a master's in urban education from Florida International University and a bachelors in fine arts (theater), from the University of Central Florida. His research interests include: institutional and systemic racism, Black relationships/partnering; and Afro-Pessimism.

Evelyn Amponsah is currently (ABD) PhD in social and political thought at York University, Canada. She is the chair of the York University Black Graduate Students' Collective. Her work is on Afro-Pessimism, Black studies, diaspora studies, social and political critiques of whiteness, popular culture, cultural studies, and love as resistance. She also works on decolonizing the academy in Ghana and Canada.

Riché Richardson is currently an associate professor of African American literature in the Africana Studies and Research Center at Cornell University from Montgomery, Alabama. Her essays have been published in various journals and books. Her first book, *Black Masculinity and the U.S. South: From Uncle Tom to Gangsta* (2007), was highlighted by Choice Books among the "Outstanding Academic Titles of 2008." Since 2005, she has served as coeditor of the New Southern Studies book series at the University of Georgia Press. She is also an artist whose mixed-media quilts have been featured in various exhibitions.

Dale Williams, a doctoral student at the University of Memphis, is pursuing a PhD in English concentrating in literary and cultural studies. With more than twenty years of experience in higher education, she is the founder of Leadership for Queens, a leadership organization for Historically Black College and University (HBCU) students. Dale received a Bachelor of Science in speech communications and theater and a Master of Arts in English from Tennessee State University. She also holds a graduate certificate in African

American literature from the University of Memphis. Dale enjoys writing about cultural aspects affecting the African American community.

Karen McMeo is an author and writer and has a Bachelor and Master of Arts degree in English. Her writing experience includes teaching college writing, book reviews, news and profile-based articles, and television scripts. Her "Letters to the Editor" have appeared in *The Washington Post*. Her self-published book, *Sincerely Yours,* garnered a favorable review from the Writer's Digest Self-Published Book Awards. In addition, she is a self-made advocate for her daughter with special needs and enjoys sharing her experiences and providing information about resources to other parents who are on a similar journey. She also enjoys dining out, going to the movies/theater, reading, exercising, and traveling.

Renata Ferdinand, PhD, is an associate professor of English at New York City College of Technology in Brooklyn, New York. She writes auto-ethnographies that explore the complexities of the lived experiences of Black women, from how race and gender impact experiences within the healthcare system to colorism, racial stereotypes, and Black women's identity. She teaches courses in both the English Department and the African American Studies Department. Currently, she is working on a book project that uses autoethnography to explore African American motherhood.

www.ingramcontent.com/pod-product-compliance
Lightning Source LLC
Chambersburg PA
CBHW022323280326
41932CB00010B/1203